Golden Touch

Blackjack Revolution!

by Frank Scoblete

Research Services Unlimited
Casino Gambling Book Publisher
6845 Highway 90E, Suite 105
Daphne, Alabama 36526
www.rsucasinobooks.com

Golden Touch Blackjack Revolution!

Address all inquires to the publisher:

Research Services Unlimited
6845 Highway 90E, Suite 105
Daphne, Alabama 36526
1-251-625-6161
Email: **info@rsucasinobooks.com**

Manufactured in the United States of America
ISBN 10: 0-912177-16-0
ISBN 13: 978-0-912177-16-8
Library of Congress Control Number: 2006901196

Cover design by Ben Jordan

Page layout and typesetting by DeepNet Technologies:
www.DeepNetTech.com

The material in this book is intended to inform and educate the reader and in no way represents an inducement to gamble legally or illegally.

To the Golden Touch Blackjack Crew

Dan Pronovost

Henry Tamburin

Dominator

Stickman

Street Dog

Table of Contents

Foreword by Frank Scoblete

Golden Touch Blackjack is the easiest advantage-play method in the world for the game of blackjack and it would not have been possible without the hard work of Dan Pronovost, who discovered Speed Count and created the Optimum Basic Strategy.

I also thank Henry Tamburin, my publisher and good friend for helping me structure the book, and last but never least, a thank you to the Dominator who convinced us all that Golden Touch Blackjack would be a great advantage-play class for players to take.

Let this book be your first step into the world of advantage blackjack play. If you practice what we teach you in this book, you will have the edge over the casinos. If you enjoy that, then consider taking our Golden Touch Blackjack class, which will make you an even stronger player (see page 155 for more details).

If you are a novice player or have very little experience playing blackjack, I encourage you to read the appendix "How to Play Blackjack" on page 147, before you start with Speed Count. You will also find a glossary of blackjack terms used in this book on page 171.

There's nothing as enjoyable as beating the casinos at their own games! Winning is the most fun!

So have some fun!

- Chapter 1 -
The Number to Change Your Blackjack Life

I want you to keep a number in your head for awhile. That number is 2.7 as in two-point-seven. Got that? The number is 2.7. This number will change your blackjack-playing life. This number might also destroy all the casinos in the world that offer blackjack if enough people read this book and/or take our advanced hands-on Golden Touch Blackjack course. So you better read this book carefully and get thee to the casinos before they disappear because we are about to reveal the simplest advantage-play method ever developed for blackjack.

Once more that's 2.7 – 2.7 – 2.7.

But first:

There are four basic types of blackjack players:

1. **The Ploppy:** This individual plays by the seat of his pants, which is sometimes called "intuition" and he will often criticize others at his table for their poor play (which could actually be proper play since the Ploppy hasn't got a clue!). The Ploppy gives the house an edge of around two to ten percent because of his bad play. The Ploppy is rife in the casinos and is lauded by the casino bosses as the type of player every casino desires – totally stupid. The Ploppy, while generally dumb, is not always dumb in real life, just dumb in casino-gambling life.

2. **Kinda Sorta Basic Strategy Player:** This player makes most of the right moves at the table, although there are certain hands that he or she misplays because the true basic strategy just doesn't seem right at any given moment. "Hit my 12 against a dealer's two? What are you crazy? The 12

brings out those 10 cards, man." These players will double for less, won't split or re-split pairs correctly and will probably be facing about a one to two percent house edge. These might just be the majority of casino blackjack players.

3. **The Basic Strategy Player:** Still a minority in the casinos, these players use the correct basic strategy for the blackjack games they like to play. The house will have about a one-half percent house edge on these players – give or take a few tenths of a percent depending on the game being played and the rules. It is actually not hard to be a Basic Strategy player as the casino gift shops sell Basic Strategy cards that you can use at the tables. The fact that so many players don't use them – so many, many players – is an indication of how rotten our education system is! If they give you a legal cheat sheet, why not use it? Duh!

4. **The Card Counter/Advantage Player:** The player the casinos hate the most because he can keep track of when the game favors him and bet accordingly. While card counting has been known for almost a half century, very few blackjack players can actually do it in the casinos. Of the nine to 10 million blackjack players in the country, there are (maybe) a few thousand who have the ability to successfully count cards in the casinos.

There is a sub category of #4, variously known as the math whiz, math weenie, mathlete and computer nerd who does all the hard stuff (hard stuff is my way of explaining all the hard stuff that actually goes into the analysis of blackjack) to figure out if this strategy gives us one-one-billionth of a percentage advantage over that strategy. You will readily identify these individuals in the casinos because they all wear little beanies with propellers on top of them. And plastic pocket protectors. But we owe them a debt of gratitude for the information they have given us even though we might not want to go out to dinner with them. The math whizzes have made blackjack a beatable game. All kidding aside, we owe them everything because they showed us that this casino game could be beaten.

Now the greatest of all the math weenies (for readers of this book and for me personally) is a man named Dan Pronovost who runs a company called DeepNet Technologies in the wilds of Canada (**www.deepnettech.com**). Now I hate Dan Pronovost because he can eat like a pig, devouring truckloads of food, and remain skinny. I mean really skinny. That is a sin against man and God and nature but some other time for all of that.

Otherwise Dan Pronovost is one hell of a guy and the man who has invented, created, and birthed the greatest discovery in blackjack history – a discovery that is going to make you an advantage player at the game by the end of chapter two of this book (Don't you dare skip this chapter! Get back here!).

Between points 3 and 4 on page 2 is a vast distance, a monstrous chasm, and an endless gulf that most blackjack players have not been able to leap, jump or get across. Going from being a Basic Strategy player to being a Card Counting advantage player is not easy; if it were, millions of blackjack players would now be playing with an edge. They aren't, and the simplest proof is that casinos still have beatable blackjack games and make a tremendous profit from them. Card counting is daunting for almost all blackjack players; many have tried it and failed at it – which makes the casino executives very happy even though they spit when they hear the words "card counter" as if such an appellation was like calling someone a mass murderer.

Even "popular counts" such as High-Low have you keeping track of the high cards (Aces and 10-valued cards) and low cards (2, 3, 4, 5 and 6). You add 1 for every small card that comes out and you subtract 1 for every big card that comes out. That's your *running* count. Next you glance at the discard tray and estimate the number of decks that have been played. You then subtract that number from the total number of decks being used which gives you the number of unplayed decks in the shoe. Then you have to divide (or in single-deck games, multiply) the number of unplayed decks of cards into the running count to get your *true* count – which tells you what your edge is. Then you bet a proportion of your edge on the next round, if the count favors you, or you bet very low or not at all if the count doesn't favor you.

Sound simple?

It might. But such mental mathnastics cause most would-be card counters to take a nosedive while attempting to play these methods in the casinos. I'm guessing you might just be one of them.

For most blackjack players card counting just isn't in their cards. It's hard to keep the count accurately, add and subtract, multiply and divide, bet properly, hand after hand, round after round and that's why the casinos have actually benefited by the card counting revolution because most of the would-be revolutionaries have died on the field (or felt) of battle. While card counting has been around for about 50 years, the success stories are few and far between.

And so it has remained. Propeller hats and a few thousand card counters out of about 10 million current blackjack players beat the game and the rest of the blackjack players, even those who are smart players playing perfect basic strategy, are losers. Casino executives are very happy about that, too.

So it has remained.

Until now that is.

Until Dan Pronovost.

Until number 2.7's dimensions were fully understood.

All current card counting systems use some form of the "count the low cards" or "count the high cards" method such as we saw with High-Low. However, Dan Pronovost was out walking in the snowy moonlight of his Canadian wilderness one night, with his trusty husky Simu (short for simulation) by his side, when a thought hit him: "Everyone knows that the average number of cards in an average blackjack hand is about two point seven, with little variance. I wonder if that means anything significant for advantage play?"

(That's the blackjack-life-changing number my dear reader – 2.7!)

After a hearty dinner of more food than you'll find at your local delicatessen, Dan went to his computer for the remainder of the long Canadian winter. And discovered something amazing, which I will summarize succinctly: Of the 2.7 cards that each player gets, about one on average will be a small card. Then Dan thought hard and long, or long and hard, in between bites of a massive hero sandwich. It is possible, he thought, that you could keep track of the small cards only – and to hell (or, as they say in socialist Canada, "to heck") with the big cards.

Voila! Open says me! Damn the torpedoes! I've hit the jackpot! Eureka!

And Dan Pronovost, skinny genius, created Speed Count, a method for getting a nice healthy edge at blackjack without any of the overwhelming burdens of the traditional card counting systems. In fact, Speed Count is so simple that even a 12-year old could learn it. And if a 12-year old can learn it then certainly you can too as most of us know how smart most 12 year olds are.

Dan was ecstatic and told his business partner, gaming's great best selling author Dr. Henry Tamburin, about the Speed Count, which at that time was called "this thing." Henry knowing a good "thing" when he heard it promptly called me and told me about "this thing." I then called Dominator about it. Now four of us knew this secret new advantage-play method, which came to be known as Speed Count and came to be incorporated into our Golden Touch Blackjack course.

Thankfully Dan had done godzillions of computer simulations of the Speed Count and we knew that it was an advantage-play method that no one had ever thought of before.

It sure worked on the computer. But how easy would it really be to use in the casinos? After all, that is the true test of any advantage-play method – does it work in the real casino wars or is it just a fancy computer-generated strategy that dies on the field of battle?

So the next step was to go into the casinos of America and test out the Speed Count. Was it as easy as we thought?

Now Henry Tamburin, Dominator and I were all High-Low card counters. Henry has been High-Lowing for over 30 years and Dominator and I for over 20 years each. That's over 70 years of successful High-Low play in the casinos of America.

We now took our new system, which you will learn in Chapter Two (again, don't you dare jump ahead!) and went into the casinos. For six months the three of us played Speed Count in casinos in Nevada, New Jersey, Mississippi, and the Midwest. Dan played it in Canada, making his way to the few casinos that populate the terrain of Canada on his trusty dogsled. We played it on single-deck games, double-deck games, 6-deck games and even 8-deck games.

The method worked – to perfection. It was easy to play. It required almost no mental energy. You could play Speed Count and talk to the pit bosses and the floor people. You could watch the games on the televisions in the casinos. You could look like a normal player. In fact, even better, you could look really stupid while playing it! All the things card counters do as they are counting the cards we didn't have to do. We could look like your average idiot, the average Ploppy – which in a casino is a good thing. Idiots are *loved* in casinos. Ploppies are worshipped. Smart players are hated. Card counters are despised. But Speed Count didn't operate like those old traditional card counting systems, so while card counters are busy counting up all the big and little cards as they come out of the shoe or deck, a Speed Counter can sip his drink and watch television or the waitress or the waiter or all three!

It was a revelation. And it was as easy as pie – mounds of which Dan also eats by the way.

In fact, Speed Count was so easy to use that the three of us, three big time High-Low players with over 70 years of experience, said to ourselves: "You know, why not play this simple method and to hell (heck) with the old ways?"

Now, Speed Count will not give you the same kind of edge as you get with the High-Low counting system but so what? If you tried High-Low and failed to be able to do it, what do you care that your edge is somewhat smaller now that you finally have an edge? Come on, you work ten and a half times as hard for your High-Low edge (I simulated that on my old slide rule) but you don't get ten and a half times the edge at it – so if Speed Count is about 50 to 75 percent as strong as High-Low (depending on the game) but is one thousand times easier (another of my simulations) to use, why not use it? You can even make just as much money per hour with Speed Count compared to High-Low, at the cost instead of a 50 to 100 percent increase in your bankroll requirements (depending on the game and rules).

You know something, you can get tired doing High-Low for a few hours at a time and you can make mistakes and, you know what, can't something be **easy** for a change? Do all good things have to be hard so only people with propeller hats and pocket protectors can do them? Hell (heck) no! Here was something that was easy; that worked; that gave a nice edge at the game. It doesn't get much better than that. And it was easy, easy, easy!

Man, I had been doing High-Low for 20 years and I realized it was time to sit back, light up a grossly expensive cigar, drink a fine non-French wine, and get an edge over the house without the work I used to do with High-Low. Speed Count was wonderful for that. In fact, I could play longer and still make the kind of money I was making playing shorter sessions on High-Low. I would also get a lot more in comps. The good life was here!

Yes, some of the old guard, those mousy-faced computer guys will snort and sniff at what good young skinny

Dan Pronovost has discovered. They will say things like, "Uh, uhm, ooo, eee, High-Low is better, ee, oww, ooo." But do you care that they think you should be playing something that most people can't learn and use? I'll answer for you – NO, YOU DON'T! If you have tried to count the traditional way and you have failed, it doesn't matter what these others think. For you, the savior has arrived and they are not him. As Ken Uston, one of the early day's great counters said, "playing a modest system perfectly is a lot better than playing a complex system poorly."

Your savior and the savior of all basic strategy players looking to become advantage players will be Speed Count coupled with our new basic strategy (called OBS for Optimum Basic Strategy), our insurance strategies, our game exit strategies, and our betting strategies. This bundle is what we call our Golden Touch Blackjack technique.

And it is all easy as pie.

Speed Count is new. Speed Count is revolutionary. Speed Count works. And Speed Count is easy to learn and easy to use. It gives you a good edge over the casino that you will be able to exploit.

Our new basic strategy (OBS) will increase the edge Speed Count gives us as will our insurance and exit strategies.

Again, easy as pie.

Glorious! Spectacular.

Long live Golden Touch Blackjack and the skinny guy who gave us Speed Count and OBS – Dan Pronovost!

- Chapter 2 -
How Speed Count Works

The key number in the Speed Count is 31. At 31 in all games, single-deck, double-deck, 4-decks, 6-decks, and 8-decks, the player will have the edge over the casino and be able to make himself some money. In blackjack terms, 31 is like 21 in drinking terms (at least where I live) as that is the age where you can drink legally and make yourself sick as a dog.

But let me go back a little in time and explain exactly what the Speed Count is. Since every player who is in the game will receive an average of 2.7 cards per hand that he plays, one of which on average will be a small card by lucky coincidence, you add up the small cards that have come out (the small cards are 2, 3, 4, 5, and 6), and you subtract the number of players or completed hands from the total.

And what is that total?

Let us take a typical two-deck game first and assume for simplicity that the cards are dealt face up. Dan Pronovost has determined through billions of computer simulations and hero sandwiches that the Speed Count for a double-deck game starts at 30. Let us say there are two players – you and a Ploppy. You also have the dealer. So you know you will subtract 3 from the Speed Count after a round. If there is a split you will subtract 4. If there are two splits you will subtract 5.

Now the dealer deals out the cards: you get a 10 and a 2; the Ploppy gets a 6 and 4; and the dealer shows a 6 as the upcard. So do you start counting the small cards right now?

No, you don't. No hand has been played.

Card counters are busily counting the big and small cards right now but you are doing nothing. You do not start counting, I'll say this again, because no hands have been played. I repeat, NO HANDS HAVE BEEN PLAYED. Now I usually don't like to use all caps as that is considered yelling when you write on a message board on the Internet but with Speed Count it is essential that you not count a small card until a hand has been played. If I have to I will put that in caps again....

What makes Speed Count different from all counting strategies is the fact that you are adding small cards and then subtracting from them the number of hands played– I repeat, the number of hands played – so if a hand is not finished, there is no counting going on. Yes, that means if a small card should fall out of the dealer's hand and is then put in the discard rack – it is not counted, as that card does not relate to a player's hand. This is not traditional card counting. I repeat, this is not traditional card counting.

Okay, let's go around the table:

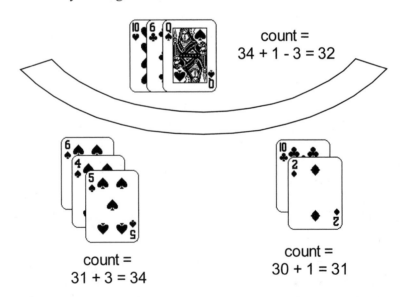

count =
34 + 1 - 3 = 32

count =
31 + 3 = 34

count =
30 + 1 = 31

You stand on your 10 and 2 against the dealer's 6. Your hand is finished. The count is now 31 – you started with 30 on the two-deck game, added one for your small card of 2, and so your Speed Count is now 31.

Now the Ploppy has to play his hand. He doubles on his 6 and 4 and gets a 5. His hand is finished. There are three small cards added to your 31 (6, 4, and 5) and the Speed Count is now at 34.

Finally the dealer turns over her hole card, a 10, and she has 16. She hits and busts with a queen. You add her small card (the 6) to the total of 34 and you now have a SC of 35.

Three hands were played, so you subtract 3 from 35 and you get 32. That is your new Speed Count, 32, and that means you have an edge over the house. I'll explain in a little while how to bet with your edges but for now just get the picture:

1. You start the two-deck game at the Speed Count of 30.

2. When a hand is finished being played, you add all the small cards in that hand to the initial Speed Count of 30. In our example we got to 35 at the end of the round.

3. When everyone has played their hands, you subtract the number of hands or players from the total to arrive at your new Speed Count. In the above example, we subtracted three hands from 35 to arrive at 32.

That's it folks; that is Speed Count.

There are none of the mathematical gymnastics you have to do with traditional card counting. From the initial Speed Count, you simply add the small cards when a player's hand is finished; then you subtract the number of hands played. Bingo! You have your new Speed Count.

Let's try it again to make sure you have it down pat. We are still playing a two-deck game played face up. The initial Speed Count starts at 30. There are five people at the table this time – four players and the dealer. (Yes, the dealer's hand counts too! Please don't forget that).

The dealer deals out the following cards (see diagram on page 13 to follow along):

Player One: 10-5

Player Two: 10-Queen

Player Three: 5-7

Player Four: 9-9

Dealer Upcard: 7

What is the count right now? It is still 30 because no hands have been played. This is the key ingredient – when the cards are being dealt out you should be doing something other than looking at all the cards. When a hand is being played then you look at the cards for that hand. This is a radical departure from traditional card counting.

Now we play the hands.

Player One hits his 10-5 and busts with a 7. You add one to the count of 30 because Player One had a small card (the 5). The Speed Count is now 31.

Player Two stands on his 20. You add nothing to the count because Player Two did not have a small card. The Speed Count is still 31.

Player Three hits his 5-7 and gets a 9. You add one. The Speed Count is now 32.

Player Four stands on his 9-9. You add nothing to the count because Player Four does not have a small card in his hand. The Speed Count is still 32.

The dealer turns over a King for a King-7 and stands. You add nothing to the count because the dealer does not have a small card. The Speed Count is still 32.

There are five hands that have been played. You subtract five from 32 and you get 27. That is your new Speed Count. The house has the edge because the Speed Count is less than 31.

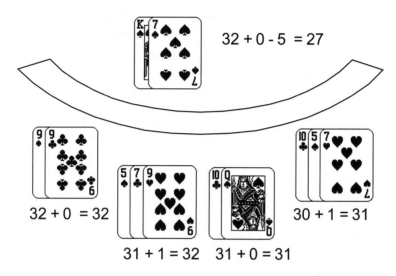

The next round begins and your Speed Count is 27. So let's deal out some more cards (see diagram on page 15):

Player One gets a 2-3

Player Two gets a 6-6

Player Three gets a 10-4

Player Four gets a 7-3

Dealer gets an upcard of 6

What is the Speed Count? It is 27! That is the count that started this round and it is still the count because no hands have been played. I repeat – NO HANDS HAVE BEEN PLAYED.

Let's play the hands.

Player One hits his 2-3 and gets a 5. He hits again and gets a 2. He now stands. He received four small cards (2, 3, 5, and 2) so you add four to 27 and the Speed Count is now 31.

Player Two splits his 6-6 against the dealer's upcard of 6. We have just added an extra hand to the game. The best thing to do is subtract this hand right now so the count is now 30. On the first hand of 6, the dealer gives the player a 9 and the player stands. You add one to the count as the player had one small card (the 6). The Speed Count is now 31. On the second 6, the dealer gives the player a 5; the player doubles and gets a jack. You now add two to the count as the player received two small cards (6 and 5). The count is now 33.

Player Three stands on his 10-4. You add one to the count as he had a small card (the 4). The Speed Count is now 34.

Player Four doubles on his 7-3 and gets a 4. He now stands. Since two small cards came out (the 3 and 4), the Speed Count goes to 36.

The Dealer turns over her hole card and she has a King underneath. She hits her King-6 and gets an 8 and busts. We add one to the count because the Dealer had one small card (the 6). The Speed Count is now 37.

We subtract the five hands (four players plus the dealer) from 37 and the Speed Count is now 32. Remember on the split we subtracted the extra hand immediately. Splits will occur about 2.5 percent of the time, so just subtracting immediately will not confuse us when we do our end-of-the-round subtraction of the number of players plus the dealer. Repeat: Subtract the split hand immediately. If I have to use caps to drive this home I will.

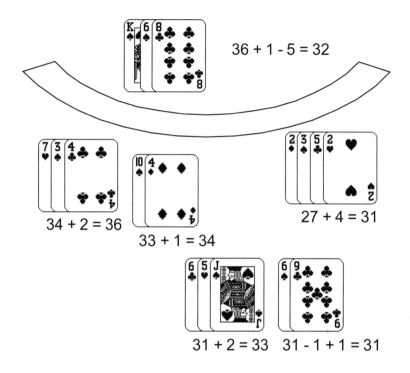

Okay, you have just learned the essentials of Speed Count. In a two-deck game, you start at 30. When you get to 31, you have an edge over the house; when you are less than 31, the house has the edge over you. It's simple as can be.

Number of Decks

Of course, not all games are two-deckers. While the bet pivot number 31 will be the same for all games and will indicate an edge at all games, the starting number for Speed Count will change based on the number of decks. Here's how to begin your Speed Count with various decks:

- **Ultimate Single-Deck Games**: with DAS (Double After Splits) and S17 (Dealer Standing on Soft 17): Speed Count Begins at 31. (Yes, you have an edge off the top in this game – if you can find this game, that is).

- **Single-Deck Games (Inferior rules):** Speed Count begins at 30.
- **All Double-Deck Games:** Speed Count begins at 30.
- **All Four-Deck Games:** Speed Count begins at 29.
- **All Six-Deck Games:** Speed Count begins at 27.
- **All Eight-Deck Games:** Speed Count begins at 26.

Obviously, the rules of the game and the penetration of the game will determine how well your edge improves at 31 – although 31 will indicate an edge in all games. If the casino allows DAS, S17, Re-splits and Surrender, your edge will improve more dramatically than in a game where the dealer hits soft 17 (H17), you can't double after splits, and you can't re-split or surrender. Still 31 is the magic number because at that number, you get the best of the casino, regardless of the rules. As you head up the scale to Speed Counts of 32, 33, 34, 35 and higher, your edge gets stronger and stronger over the casino.

The reverse is also true. At 30, the casino has a slight edge in all but the most player-favorable games. In good games (DAS, Re-splits, S17, and Surrender) that edge is smaller than at bad games (no DAS, no Re-splits, H17, and no Surrender). As you go down the scale to 29, 28, 27, 26, 25 and lower, the house edge becomes stronger and stronger over you. See page 32 for a nice graph that shows this.

Face Up and Face Down Games

Some new advantage-play blackjack players get themselves in a state of high anxiety because they think that games which are dealt face down – meaning you can't see the other players' cards until he or she busts or the dealer turns them over at the end – makes Speed Count harder to do. Nothing is further from the truth.

It doesn't matter that the cards are face down on the table. You aren't counting cards, you are counting hands played and adding small cards, and, again, the small cards are not counted until the hand is played. In face down games, when a player busts, his cards are turned over. The dealer takes his money and then his cards. You have plenty of time to add the small cards in the busted hand when this happens.

At the end, when the dealer turns over his cards, you add the small cards in his hand. Then the dealer goes from player to player, turning over the cards, seeing what the hand is, paying or taking the bets. That's when you add the small cards.

No dealer is so fast that you can't add the small cards. In a normal blackjack game the hand is not quicker than the eye. That saying is only true in magic or cheating.

Face-up games are just a little more orderly but, regardless, Speed Counting face down games is quite easy. Since most of the better games are dealt from double-decks, these are usually (although not always) dealt face down.

Why Such High Speed Count Numbers?

Now, you might want to know why Dan Pronovost and Henry Tamburin decided to use the number 31 and other numbers in that range for Speed Count. All the other count systems use much lower numbers and also minus (negative) numbers. There are two reasons why we kept our numbers high. Here is the first reason:

Henry Tamburin: *Most fledgling card counters have difficulty mentally adding and subtracting positive and negative integers, which is required in most traditional card counting systems. It's easy to add +4 to a +2 and get a +6. But what does +2 added to a -5 equal? How about adding -7 to a +3? To make the chance of having to deal with negative integers with Speed Count virtually zero, the pivot point was set at 31 and the initial Speed Count (ISC) was set at 30 (single and double-deck), 29 (four-decks), 27 (six-decks), and 26 (eight-decks). Another benefit is regardless of the number of decks,* players who use Speed Count know that the edge shifts from the house to the player as soon as the Speed Count increases to 31 or higher. The key number in blackjack is 21; with Speed Count it's 31.

Here is the second reason:

Dominator: *Sometimes you might be playing at the same table with another Speed Counter, which we'll talk about later in this book, and one of you loses the count. If you ask your playing partner what he thinks the weather in Alaska is right now and he says, "I heard it was 33 degrees," well you know what the Speed Count is. It is rare that normal counting systems ever get their counts into such high numbers and the casino pits are not trained to hear those high numbers. Everything we have done with Speed Count is to make it react unlike all the other counting systems. That's right, we want you to be doing what other advantage blackjack players don't do. The casinos have trained themselves to hunt and destroy traditional card counters. Well, Speed Counters are not going to look much like those traditional counters. So we put our numbers higher partly for that purpose.*

- Chapter 3 -
Betting Your Count

2, 4, 6, 8, 10, 12...

When the edge favors the casino you want to bet small (or not at all) but when the edge favors you, you'll want to bet big. An advantage player at blackjack has to get the money on the table when the game favors him. It's the only way to win in the long run. Getting the money on the table in "good" counts (also called "high" counts) makes up for the steady losses you get when the game favors the house. In the next chapter, I'll discuss the kind of edges you can get with the Speed Count strategies outlined here but right now I am going to give you three methods of betting for each game: conservative, aggressive, and super aggressive.

I will use the phrase "units" in describing how to bet. Your unit can be $5, $10, $12.50, $20, $25, $100 and so on. You determine what a unit is. Units can be an awkward amount and not just an even amount. If you want your unit to be 27 dollars, that's fine. The betting recommendations coming up are just that – recommendations. You can bet more if you want, although I would not recommend betting more in low "good" counts since your edge at 31 is smallish no matter what game you are playing. As long as you are betting your smallest amount when the count is 30 or lower, and more when the Speed Count is 31 or higher, then you will be playing profitably.

Insurance

Never take insurance! That's a dictum given to basic strategy players and for them it is a truism. For you, the truth lies elsewhere. Insurance can be a good thing for the Speed Counter when used properly. Thus, there will also be a number given at which insurance is a bet that gives you an edge. To insure properly, you must do the counting exactly as described in tables a bit later on. Some players like to flip the Speed Counting upside down and do the subtraction of the number of hands from the Speed Count at the start of the round, followed by the addition of the small cards as hands are played. But that can get very confusing for the insurance decisions since these are based on the past and not the future count. This technique for insurance is also quite different than what traditional card counters do in trying to exploit the insurance bet. Traditional card counters are very concerned with the cards that have just come out when the dealer shows an ace. Those of you playing Golden Touch Blackjack are not concerned with the cards that have just come out because **no hands have been played.**

How much improvement in performance does taking insurance at the recommended Speed Count provide? From the tables after page 136, we can see that the base expectation using Speed Count Conservative for a two-deck game, one player, DAS/S17 is 0.4909 percent. If we take insurance at the recommended Speed Count of 34 and higher, our edge increases to 0.5127 percent, a performance boost of 4.4 percent. The increase is even less significant as you play with more decks, and will occur less often. Never accepting insurance is often good camouflage, so you might want to consider this in four or more deck games, given the nominal performance benefit.

Golden Touch Exit Strategies

The lower the Speed Count goes, the worse it is for the advantage-play Golden Toucher. There are counts that you'd like to sit out and not bet on every round because the casino's edge is ridiculously high and we will indicate what these counts are as well. Now, you can sit out all the counts in this range or just some of them some of the time. Remember you don't want the floor person or pit boss to notice that you sit out too many hands (when the Speed Count is low) because that is a technique that card counters often use. Sitting out some of them is a good thing to do though. You can go to the bathroom on one low count; get a cell phone call on another low count (make sure your phone is off so it doesn't ring as you are pretending to talk into it), or just sit out a hand as players will sometimes do. Selecting when to sit out helps increase your edge in the game. Playing in the really low, low counts hurts your bankroll.

The Bottom Line

It is our opinion that if you use the conservative method of betting we recommend, then the casinos will have a very difficult time getting a bead on the fact that you have an advantage. In fact, at 31 we Golden Touchers find an edge that most other card counting systems don't usually see. Therefore we are upping our bet before the traditional card counters will be upping their bets. As the counts go higher than 31, the traditional counting systems and Speed Count will reflect each other much more closely. But at 31, chances are that our bets will be increased and the traditional counters bet might just be his initial low bet.

However, if you become a more aggressive bettor, especially those of you betting green, black and purple (or higher) chips, the casino will scrutinize your play much more closely since you are jumping your bets considerably and the total amount of the money being wagered is rather large. If you use the super aggressive strategies, you might find that some casinos might ask you not to play. Treading cautiously is a wise way to go – especially as you get the feel of what it is like to actually be playing a game that can beat the casinos, which you will be doing with our Golden Touch strategies.

Playing for at most 30 minutes to 45 minutes when you bet aggressively is the best advice we can give you. You don't want the casinos to get a good bead on you. Conservative bettors can probably play much longer in the same casino compared to aggressive players who must hit and run.

Speed Count Betting for Different Games

The following tables summarize the Speed Count metrics for all the different blackjack games. They are categorized by number of decks. The rules of the game (i.e., doubling after splits or dealer hits/stands on soft 17) do not matter for these metrics. And most important, for all games the magic bet pivot is 31, which is when you have the advantage and should start betting more.

As you play with more decks, the casino has an inherent increasing advantage over you. This is why the starting count is lower for these games.

The bet spread row tells you what to bet at each Speed Count value. For example, '< 31: 1' means bet one unit when the count is 30 or less. '>= 34: 5' means bet 5 units when the count is 34 or higher. '33: 4' means bet 4 units when the count is exactly 33. The more conservative the betting strategy the lower the spread between your minimum bet and maximum bet. For example, in a 2-deck game, the conservative betting strategy uses a 1 to 4 bet spread while the aggressive betting strategy uses 1 to 5.

The hand spreading row applies only to the "very aggressive" strategy (see page 24). This means that at very high counts, you play more than one hand. It is very important to note that you do **not** divide your top bets, but instead are doubling (or tripling) them. For example, in a two-deck game the bet spread calls for 5 units at a count of 34 or higher. And the hand spreading calls for 2 hands at a count of 34. Then when the count is 34, you will play two hands with 5 bet units on each (**not** 2.5 bet units on each).

We've provided three different playing styles in the columns: conservative, aggressive and very aggressive. Conservative strategy will earn you the least money, but also will attract the least attention from the casino pit bosses. Aggressive style adds a slightly higher bet spread, exit strategy, and insurance. The Very Aggressive strategy adds hand spreading and definitely represents the kind of play that will attract attention from the casino, therefore you must play with extreme caution and for short durations! As well as the added attention, the very aggressive strategy means much higher bankroll risk, since you are betting so much more money when the count is favorable (see page 67).

While your advantage (edge) goes up the more the count is greater than 31, it is also true that the casino's edge goes up as the count drops. At some point then, it makes sense to simply stop playing when the count is very low. The "exit game" counts listed in the tables are when you should simply stop playing hands, until the Speed Count goes back up (i.e., don't play when the count is 26 or less in a two-deck game). Talk up your bad luck or changing the order of the cards, take a bathroom break, check your phone, order a drink, whatever it takes to sit out a few hands. Even if you have to sit out the remainder of the shoe, it's better to stop playing at these low counts. Sitting out hands is considered a bit more aggressive since casinos sometimes discourage the practice or don't allow mid-shoe entry and will post a sign at the table stating this.

Smart basic strategy players know that insurance is a losing bet. But when the count is sufficiently high, things turn around and it makes sense to accept insurance. Accept insurance when the Speed Count is equal to or greater than the listed counts in the table (e.g., at 34 or greater in a two-deck game).

Single-Deck Games

Single-Deck	Conservative / Simple	Aggressive	Very Aggressive
Starting count	30 or 31[1]		
Bet spread (count: units)	• < 30: 1 • 31: 2 • >= 32: 3	• < 30: 1 • 31: 2 • 32: 3 • >= 33: 4	
Hand spreading (count: # hands)	NEVER	NEVER	• 32: 2 • >= 33: 3
Exit game	OPTIONAL (<= 27)	<= 27	<= 27
Accept insurance	OPTIONAL (>= 33)	>= 33	>= 33

Double-Deck Games

Double-Deck	Conservative / Simple	Aggressive	Very Aggressive
Starting count	30		
Bet spread (count: units)	• < 31: 1 • 31: 2 • >= 32: 4	• < 31: 1 • 31: 2 • 32: 3 • 33: 4 • >= 34: 5	
Hand spreading (count: # hands)	NEVER	NEVER	• 34: 2 • >= 36: 3
Exit game	OPTIONAL (<= 26)	<= 26	<= 26
Accept insurance	OPTIONAL (>= 34)	>= 34	>= 34

---

[1] Use 31 only for DAS/S17 games (double after splits allowed, dealer stands on soft 17), a rare case where you have the positive edge right from the start.

Four-Deck Games

Four-Decks	Conservative / Simple	Aggressive	Very Aggressive
Starting count	29		
Bet spread (count: units)	• < 31: 1 • 31: 2 • 32: 3 • 33: 4 • >= 34: 5	• < 31: 1 • 31: 2 • 32: 4 • 33: 6 • >= 34: 8	
Hand spreading (count: # hands)	NEVER	NEVER	• 35: 2 • >= 37: 3
Exit game	OPTIONAL (<= 23)	<= 23	<= 23
Accept insurance	OPTIONAL (>= 37)	>= 37	>= 37

Six-Deck Games

Six-Decks	Conservative / Simple	Aggressive	Very Aggressive
Starting count	27		
Bet spread (count: units)	• < 31: 1 • 31: 2 • 32: 4 • >= 33: 8	• < 31: 1 • 31: 2 • 32: 4 • 33: 6 • 34: 10 • >= 35: 12	
Hand spreading (count: # hands)	NEVER	NEVER	• 35: 2 • >= 39: 3
Exit game	OPTIONAL (<= 21)	<= 21	<= 21
Accept insurance	OPTIONAL (>= 38)	>= 38	>= 38

Eight-Deck Games

Eight-Decks	Conservative / Simple	Aggressive	Very Aggressive
Starting count	26		
Bet spread (count: units)	• < 31: 1 • 31: 2 • 32: 4 • 33: 6 • 34: 8 • >= 35: 10	• < 31: 1 • 31: 2 • 32: 4 • 33: 6 • 34: 10 • >= 35: 12	
Hand spreading (count: # hands)	NEVER	NEVER	• 35: 2 • >= 40: 3
Exit game	OPTIONAL (<= 20)	<= 20	<= 20
Accept insurance	OPTIONAL (>= 40)	>= 40	>= 40

Another word of caution is warranted here. Using the very aggressive strategies will bring a lot of attention on you so if you feel this is the method of play you'd like to use, then you mustn't stay more than a half hour in the game before moving on. Even though Speed Count is something new and revolutionary, jumping your bets into the stratosphere will bring attention to you.

Question: What if I want to play conservatively but also want to use the insurance bet metric and maybe sit out some hands in bad counts?

Frank Scoblete: Do it. You can mix and match the different levels of play. Most of the conservative players that I know use the insurance bet and exit strategy. Some will make their spread 1 unit to 6 units in 2-deck games. You have to decide what is best for you and what you feel you can get away with.

- Chapter 4 -
About, Around, Approximately

0.679324765

Okay, this is the chapter that is going to drive the propeller hats crazy as I am going to talk about things using the words "about," "in general," "around," and "approximately". Which means there aren't going to be decimal places to the fortieth entity (my math word). Instead I want to give you an idea of how strong Speed Count is without also giving you a severe headache in the bargain. However, if your pens are now frothing in your pocket protectors, relax, because Dan Pronovost, your new deity, will have reams of decimalized information at the end of the book that you can devour the way he devours chocolate cream pies (see page 133). He'll go nuts with math for you and computer simulations and everything that makes life worth living for those who have become one with their slide rules (are those used any more?) and computers. You will salivate with all the math and simulations you'll see there.

Speed Count and Basic Strategy

A basic strategy player using one of the casino basic strategy cards or one of the basic strategies from any good blackjack book will be playing against about (about! about! about! – is this killing you?) a half-percent house edge. That means he will lose around 50 cents for every $100 he bets.

If you are a $10 basic strategy player, you will lose approximately (approximately, approximately, approximately) $5 per hour. I'm assuming you will be playing around 100 hands per hour. Losing $5 per hour is not so outrageous considering a Megabucks slot player can lose around $400 per hour pumping in three dollars per spin.

Still basic strategy players are losers.

A conservative $10 Speed Counter will win about $7.50 per hour, in common double and six deck games with good penetration (DAS/S17 for six-deck, and DAS/H17 for double deck). Chew on that! You can lose $5 per hour as a basic strategy player or you can win $7.50 per hour as a Speed Counter (that's a $12.50 turn around). Hmmm. Which do you want to do?

Now obviously because you are raising your bets in good counts, the average bet of a Speed Counter is higher than the average bet of the Basic Strategy player but those bets are only raised when you have the edge – not when the casino has the edge. But the unit bet size below refers to the minimum bet the Speed Counter makes, not their average bet size.

Let's make a chart based on the "base" bet to see what you will win if you bet certain amounts:

Base unit bet size in dollars	Basic Strategy loss / hour	Speed Counter win / hour
$10	($5.00)	+$7.50
$15	($7.50)	+$11.25
$20	($10.00)	+$15.00
$25	($12.50)	+$18.75
$50	($25.00)	+$37.50
$100	($50.00)	+$75.50
$200	($100.00)	+$150.00
$500	($250.00)	+$375.00

The Speed Counter clearly wins a nice amount of money per hour using a conservative approach (a good rule of thumb is you will win 75 percent of your unit bet size per hour in the long run, assuming one hundred hands per hour and good rules). Additional win rates and data for the more aggressive

Speed Count version are available in the appendix (see page 133).

Average Bets

Now as I stated, a $10 Speed Counter does not have an average bet of $10. In fact, since he is raising his bets in good counts, and also doubling and splitting in all counts, his average bet per round is approximately $25. The Basic Strategy player is actually betting about $11 per hour because of splits and double downs.

While average bet size is important for bankroll sizing, it is not something that should scare you. In fact, your comps are going to go up since your average bet has gone up (see page 94 for more on comps). If you wish to be a conservative player, your bankroll does not have to be massive to allow you to play with confidence that you won't get wiped out if a bad streak hits you. And, by the way, you will get hit with bad streaks. We all do.

Maybe I should pause here to tell you about the fact that even as an advantage player you can lose – and lose and lose. Yes, your overall expectation will be positive but like even the best fighters who ever lived, you are going to take some shots to the head. Get used to that idea. You will win in the long run but you can (and will) take your lumps even as an advantage player.

Here's a story to let you know what you can experience:

Dominator: *We taught John, a black chip player, the Speed Count in a private Golden Touch Blackjack class and he was adept at it within a half hour. We also taught him a new basic strategy (Optimum Basic Strategy) and other techniques to protect him against casino heat. He went to the casinos the very next week and won $200,000 in three days. He was in heaven as he had lost millions in his blackjack-playing career up to that time.*

We all cautioned John that he was experiencing a hot streak, what the math boys call a positive fluctuation, and that he could expect a negative fluctuation as well. When it would happen we couldn't predict but that it would happen we could predict – it is always going to happen. You don't win every session even when you have the edge because that edge is tiny.

When John revisited the casinos a few weeks later, he hit the wall. He lost three days in a row - $40,000, $30,000 and $30,000. He was crestfallen. He was disheartened. He said he was losing confidence in the Speed Count and that maybe it didn't work and he should go back to playing his old way.

The way he used to play had lost him millions too! But when you get discouraged you tend to return to what brought you to the Speed Count in the first place – lousy losing strategies!

John was completely wrong on this – obviously. He had won $200,000; lost $100,000. The Speed Count was working fine. He was also in a very short run. Thankfully, John had a small winning streak and now regained his confidence in the Speed Count. But those losing days had thrown him. Let me say this for everyone to hear: people you can have losing sessions, days, weeks and maybe even months despite the fact that you have the edge.

Frank once lost 20 hands in a row. Both Henry and I were at the same table with him when this happened. I've gone days where I can't buy a win. So has Henry. So has Dan. It is the nature of the game for you to have ups and downs but over time your ups will win out if you play properly. Don't panic if you lose. You have the edge but that edge is small. As Frank says, you will have to get used to the fact that you will be taking some lumps. But a basic strategy player takes many more lumps and is a loser in the end. That's the big difference. A Golden Toucher is a winner; all the others are losers. When a bad streak occurs, say that in your mind: I am a winner. I will play perfectly. I am a winner. Don't play scared.

What is My Edge?

In the Appendix on page 133, Dan Pronovost has reams of information about the whole range of edges that you can get with Speed Count at the various games using conservative and aggressive strategies. But some rules of thumb apply and you should know these. You don't have to memorize Dan's charts but you should acquaint yourself with certain facts about the edge at blackjack.

The edge with Speed Count can go from one-tenth of one percent (you win a dime for every $100 you wager) to 1.5 percent (you win $1.50 for every $100 you wager). Of course, to get that 1.5 percent you must be a super-aggressive player, something that is really not recommended for most readers of this book, and you must be playing games with deep penetration and great rules with a sufficient bankroll.

At the bottom end, the one-tenth of one percent, are games with six or more players and horrible rules with no DAS and dealers hitting soft 17 (including many decks or poor penetration). I don't even recommend that you play in such lousy games, in fact I discourage it, but if you have to play, a conservative strategy will yield, as expected, a very small return. Yes, as bad as it is, it is still better than being a basic strategy player and much better than being a Ploppy.

In fact, you will probably be playing games and strategies somewhere between these two extremes. Your edge will probably be around one-half percent, give or take a tenth of a percent. This is damn good considering the effort needed to attain this edge is very small.

How Often Will I Hit Various Counts?

The chart on page 32 shows your edge at different Speed Counts, in a traditional two-deck game (DAS, S17, 4 players, 67 percent penetration). Dan developed the chart by collecting the win/loss information from his simulations of Speed Count, and aggregating the data by the count at the start of the round. The important thing to notice is that your edge improves as the count increases, and the point where it goes from negative to positive is right between 30 and 31, which is the pivot point where we increase our bets using Speed Count.

Your Edge by Speed Count (2 decks, DAS, S17)

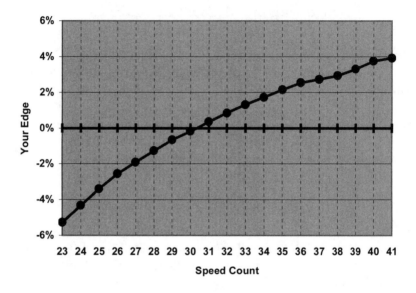

Now the next question is how often can I expect to get hands at different counts? Once again Dan went back to his simulations and sandwiches and developed the nifty histogram on page 33, which shows the highest frequency of counts centered on 30, as expected, in a two deck game (the starting Speed Count). These basic characteristics are what the propeller heads look for in a good blackjack count system, and Speed Count has it in spades.

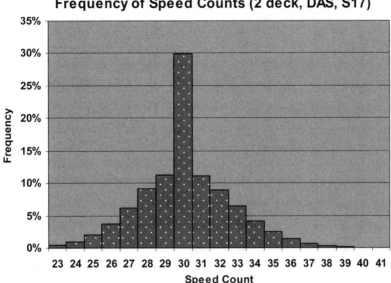

Frequency of Speed Counts (2 deck, DAS, S17)

What about more decks, more players, bad rules, less players... do these changes effect the results? Well, your edge will go up or down depending on the positive factors (less decks, better rules), but the overall principles stay the same. Your edge follows increases with the count, becoming positive around 30 or 31, and the frequency of hands is a classic bell curve shape around the starting Speed Count (i.e., the six deck game would 'hump' around 27).

Good Games and Bad Games

I wrote a sentence almost two decades ago but it bears rewriting: *Not all blackjack games are created equal.* Some games are good; some games are bad; and many games are in-between those extremes. There are two ingredients that determine whether a game is good or bad, the rules of the game and the penetration – with penetration being the much stronger element of the two.

So what is penetration? Take a deck of 52 cards and deal out 26 of the cards. That is penetration of 50 percent. It's good penetration for single-deck, but 50 percent penetration in 4 or more decks is very bad. Take two decks of cards and deal out all but 13. That is penetration of 75 percent, which is pretty good for double-deck games.

The rule about penetration applies to all blackjack games – the deeper the penetration the better it is for you because the more cards you get to play the more frequently you will encounter the higher counts. And while 50 to 66 percent penetration is acceptable (and common) for single-deck and double-deck games respectively, you'll need to find 75 percent penetration or more in 6 and 8-deck games to get a reasonable edge. If the penetration is 75 percent or above, that is good; but if the penetration is hovering near 50 percent that is bad. Can you win at games where the penetration is 50 percent? Yes, there are many games that you can beat where the penetration is 50 percent but your edge at these games is smaller than the edge you would get with that exact same game in terms of rules but with 75 percent penetration.

Most good single-deck games have shallow penetration, as casinos are paranoid about card counters beating their most vulnerable games. In the old days you could find many casinos that dealt out 75 percent of a single-deck game. Today those games are rare and 50 percent penetration (or less) is extant among the single deckers. In fact nowadays most casinos use the Rule of Six on single-deck games which defines the penetration. The Rule of Six is the number of rounds dealt plus the number of playing spots equal 6. Assuming each player is playing one spot, most casinos would deal four rounds to two players or five rounds to one player. Any penetration greater than the Rule of Six would be a great game for Speed Count (provided the rules are also satisfactory).

Most double-deck games that are playable have penetration of about 60 to 66 percent, although you can find double-deck games with 75 percent penetration if you look for them. At the minimum you should have at least 66 percent penetration.

While four-deck games are not the norm in casinos, as most casinos prefer six-deck games, the casinos that offer four-decks will usually give penetration between 60 and 75 percent.

On six- and eight-deck games, the penetration is usually 66 to 75 percent. Some casinos offer excellent six-deck games with penetration of 83 percent (one deck cut out of play) and these would be the preferred games in this variety. With both six- and eight-deck games, you have to practice patience, as the shoe will go positive less often than in a single- or double-deck game. There will be long stretches where you will be betting your minimum number of units. If you don't have patience or if your inner gambler eggs you to increase your bet when you don't have the edge, you will again belong to the loser group – the casino's favorite people! Single- and double-deck games are more explosive as the counts vary wildly. But those big shoe games are slow movers. So patience is the key for them.

Let's see how penetration affects your edge in typical two-deck and six-deck games with four players at the table (DAS, S17, 67 and 75 percent penetration for the 2 and 6 deck games respectively). We are using the conservative Speed Count strategy for these tables.

Conservative Speed Count: 6 decks	
Penetration	Edge
5/6 of shoe (83%)	0.4814%
3/4 of shoe (75%)	0.3721%
2/3 of shoe (67%)	0.2974%
1/2 of shoe (50%)	0.1604%

Conservative Speed Count: 2 decks	
Penetration	Edge
5/6 of shoe (83%)	0.6596%
3/4 of shoe (75%)	0.5452%
2/3 of shoe (67%)	0.4604%
1/2 of shoe (50%)	0.3057%

And, for those that prefer to see the above data in a graph:

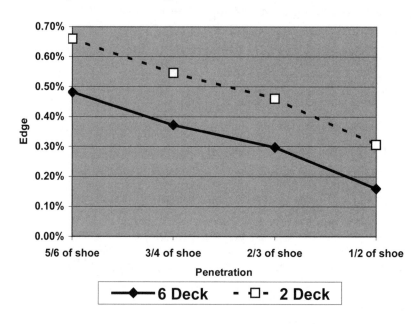

While you still have an edge at both games when 50 percent (or one half) of the cards are kept out of play, that edge is much smaller than the edge you get at five-sixths or three-fourths penetration. So while both the two and six-deck games are beatable even with a 50 percent cut, your expectation and hourly win rate is reduced markedly if you play these games.

To summarize, when using Speed Count seek out games with at *least* the following penetration:

- Single-deck – Rule of Six or higher

- 2-deck – 66 percent

- 4-deck – 70 percent

- 6/8-deck – 75 percent

Good Rules

The next ingredient in good games is good rules. Given a choice, you should always play blackjack and use Speed Count in games which have a preponderance of good rules. Here is a list of the good rules:

- Blackjack pays 3 to 2
- Insurance offered at 2 to 1 (insurance is sometimes good for Speed Counters)
- Double down on any first two cards
- Splitting any pairs
- Re-split any pairs
- Double down after pair splitting
- Split aces more than once
- Surrender (Early surrender is best, but very rare)
- Dealer stands on Soft 17 (S17)
- Entering game allowed mid-shoe

Bad Rules

Here are the bad rules:

- Blackjack pays 6 to 5 (or, worse, only even money)
- No doubling down on any first two cards
- Doubling only on 10 or 11
- No doubling down on soft hands
- No pair splitting
- No re-splitting of pairs
- No doubling down allowed after splits
- Dealer hits soft 17 (H17)
- No mid-shoe entry allowed

Games where blackjack pays 6 to 5 cannot be beaten and should be avoided. This is a rule that devours players' bankrolls. If you bet $10 and get a blackjack, at a normal game you get paid $15 for your $10 wager. At the 6-to-5 games, you get paid $12 for a blackjack. The casino keeps the other three dollars! Never, never, NEVER play games where the house pays 6 to 5 for blackjacks.

You will find that many casinos have some good rules and some bad rules on the very same game. You might be able to double down on any first two cards, split and re-split, and double down after splits. That's good. However, the game has the dealer hitting his soft 17s. That's bad. You try to get as many good rules as you can.

Given a deeply penetrated game with mediocre rules or a game that is poorly penetrated with good rules, you should opt for the deeply penetrated one. Recheck the penetration charts and see how powerful the element of penetration is. The deeper you go into the cards, the better your chance to hammer the casinos.

Those Infernal Shuffle Machines

There are two types of shuffling machines – one good (automatic shufflers), one bad (continuous shufflers). The good ones are those that shuffle a new shoe on the side while another shoe is being used so that the new shoe is ready immediately without the dealer having to spend time shuffling the decks by hand. This makes the game faster for you and fast is good since you have the edge and the more decisions you play the better it is for you in the long run.

The bad machines are called "continuous shuffle machines." There are no new shoes. There are no new rounds. The machine keeps shuffling the cards – endlessly. When a round is finished, the dealer dumps the played cards into the machine, which just shuffles them into the pack. There is no way to get an edge on continuous shuffling machines and like those 6-to-5 blackjack games, all games using such machines must be avoided.

- Chapter 5 -
We Want You to Be Stupid Like a Gorilla

85 to 95

When you were in school, the stupid kids wanted everyone else to be as stupid as they were. They had this thing about freely sharing their un-sublime idiocy. In fact, even if you didn't want to share in their stupidity and idiocy, they kind of made you because they disrupted classes, acted like fools in the hallways and cafeteria, and picked on people. Bullies were generally stupid. The stupid kids were hard to escape and they seemed to be everywhere. Today you see them driving like nuts on the various roadways of America but unless you are a teacher, you really don't have to react to the stupid kids who are as abundant today as they have always been.

As an adult you are free to only hang out with adults who meet your intellectual and emotional needs. That's a good thing. Of course, if you are a teacher...our prayers are with you!

The smart kids, on the other hand, really did not try to make anyone else smart; they just went about the singular business of getting a good education and, for most of them, becoming successful in life. For some peculiar reason secular evangelism among the young is reserved for the boneheads and not the brains.

Dominator, Henry, Dan and I are glad that you are smart. We are glad that you have decided to become an advantage player at blackjack and that you are reading this book to build a solid foundation with our Golden Touch methods of advantage play. We are also glad that some of you will decide to take our Golden Touch Blackjack class where we will teach you additional things we have learned in our combined 100 years of playing in just two days of intense training. You'll be a casino *killer* then.

Yes, it's great to be smart! Rejoice! Be happy! Big smile now! In the real world smart is good. Unfortunately, stupid is widespread; smart is rare.

Now forget all about the fact that you are smart because right now I want you to recall the jerks you went to high school with. Dig into your memory banks and look into their dull faces, their lackluster eyes and see their beetle brows. Because we want you to become as stupid as they were (and probably still are) because the casinos are like high school with neon – they are dominated by the dopes. From slot machine to executive suite, stupidity is rewarded in the casinos. Smart players are despised; dopes are lionized.

The advice we are going to give you in this chapter will make you appear to be a dope, a dullard, a moron – a Ploppy of immense magnitude and unimportance.

Start drooling!

Indeed, if you can learn to drool while you play that would be very helpful as it would make you look like a complete cretin and also make other players avoid playing at the same table with you – which is a very good thing for an advantage player. The fewer the players at the table with you, the better it is for you.

Now the advice that is coming is good advice – and it will help you maintain a nice edge over the house and give you the appearance that you are not one of the swiftest of the bunch.

Where to Sit

Think quickly – which is the best seat to be at on a blackjack table? If you know anything about traditional card counting, you will snap back, "Third base!" That's the position that is last to get his cards. For traditional card counters, third base is the best position. But for Golden Touchers doing Speed Count, third base is not the best position to be at – **first base is the best position!** You want to get your hand first. Thus first base allows you to play your hand and spend the rest of the time adding the small cards without worrying about figuring out your hand and having two numbers in your head – the total of your hand and the Speed Count.

The casino pit people are trained to suspect competent players at third base of being card counters. If you play at first base, especially if only you and one or two players are at the table, you won't look very suspicious. You benefit when you use Speed Count because your best position at the table makes you appear to be just like another Ploppy.

Don't Watch Cards As the Dealer Deals

I mentioned this before but it bears repeating – *do not watch the cards as they are being dealt out.* You can watch your own hand, that's normal, but ignore all the other hands. Talk to the floor person when the dealer is dealing. Henry Tamburin has a way of being so boring when he talks to the floor person that these characters flee him as if he has a plague – which he does, the plague of Ploppiness. While the casinos love the stupid people, individual casino people don't want to have long conversations with the Ploppy brigades. That stands to reason; after all who wants to talk to stupid people? You had to do that in high school.

Don't Add Up Other Hands

The Speed Count has just gone to 24 and you are adding up the dealer's hand. She has a 14 and takes a hit, gets an 8 for a 22. Hooray, she busted with 22! Uh, what's the count? Hmmm? Is it 22 or something else? Damn, I lost it adding up the dealer's hand!

Or I lost it adding up another player's hand.

So why are you adding up their totals? Does it help you play your hand? No, it doesn't. Does it help you keep the Speed Count? No it doesn't. Does it do any good at all? No, it doesn't. The totals of the hands of other players and the dealer are irrelevant to you. There is only one number you should be keeping in your head and that number is the Speed Count.

When hands are finished, you don't care what total the player has or if the player busted or if the player plays jingle bells on his toes – you just want to know what the Speed Count is based on the small cards that have appeared as the hands go by. Adding up the hands of the other players is a waste of time and usually a very confusing waste of time. Let the other players add their own hands and let the dealer add her own hands, too. You just keep the count and then do that final subtraction at the end of the round.

Once the count is in your head you don't want any other numbers interfering with it. Almost all other players are busy adding other players' and the dealer's hands. Good. Let them. You are so stupid you don't even care what the other players get on their hands. How's that? You don't even care what the dealer gets on his hand. The hell with the hands!

Just keep the Speed Count. Follow this advice and it serves a dual purpose. You keep the count better and you look like an ubber-Ploppy because you don't seem all that interested in what's going on in the game that you're risking money at.

Henry Tamburin: *It's no surprise that casinos love stupid players. To give the perception that I am a stupid player I will sometimes make a few faux pas in procedures that will illicit a rebuke from the dealer. In face-down hand held games I might pick up both initial cards dealt to me with two hands or not turn over my cards when I double down. In face up games, handling your cards during a pair split will often label you as a clueless player. How you place your chips in the betting circle also gives you an opportunity to play stupid. Put a higher denomination chip on top of a smaller denomination chip and the dealer and fellow players will shake their* *head. Better yet when the dealer places your winning chips next to your original chips leave them as is in the betting circle for the next hand if the count warrants.*

When it comes your turn to cut the deck after a shuffle, position the cut card three or four cards from the top or bottom of the deck(s) (it doesn't matter where you place the cut card, but it is frowned upon to cut near the top or end). I also have my trusty strategy card in my hand or place it on the layout in full view of everyone (especially the floor person). I will on occasion give a perplexed look when dealt a "tough" hand and ask my fellow players or the dealer on advice on how to play it. Better yet if the floor supervisor is at the table, I'll ask him by name, "Joe, what does the book say to play this hand?" Do that two different times with the same floor supervisor and you'll never see him again at your table.

Clueless players seem to think blackjack is a team sport while they have fun losing their money. So I join in their fun by congratulating the anchor player when his smart play "saved the table," or I'll root loudly for the dealer's draw card to be a bust card when she has to draw with a stiff hand. When the dealer breaks I cheer and clap just like my fellow players do. I'll also commiserate with a fellow player when he gets a bad beat draw and loses his bet. I'll also piss and moan loudly when I lose a hand due to a miracle draw by the dealer and state loudly, "Sue, you are killing me!"

Sitting out a few hands when the count goes south also gives me the opportunity to "help" my fellow players fortunes by smartly saying, "I'm going to sit out a few hands to change the flow of the cards" Of course using the OBS card (see page 53) has several plays different from what a normal basic strategy player would do so it sometimes brings a response from the dealer along the lines, "Are you sure you want to double on that hand?" My comeback is, "That's what my strategy card says to do and I got it from my brother-in-law and he never loses."

To reach the pinnacle of stupidity, when the floor supervisor is within earshot I often make a comment after losing a few consecutive hands such as, "I can never win at this game. I guess I'm just not lucky with cards."

The Koko Factor

Let's take a small break from the training you are being given to discuss more general realms of stupidity in the casinos from both the management side and the players' side. I will use Koko, a very famous gorilla, as the central character of what is coming up. You can relax now and just read. We'll get to more heavy material after the Koko Factor.

Now, Koko is the lowland gorilla who supposedly has an IQ of between 85 and 95; based on an IQ test she took several years back. The average range for humans is 90-110. About 50 percent of the human population in America falls within that range, with about 25 percent above it and 25 percent below it. So Koko is, by our standards, a kind of dull normal individual but she is, let's be frank, smarter than about 25 percent of the human population, which definitely includes the kid across the street from me and, perhaps, that strange neighbor of yours and most of the kids you went to high school with.

Now, I don't know if Koko is a smart gorilla or a stupid gorilla. For all I know, the average gorilla might have an IQ substantially higher than Koko's but I do know this – if a human with Koko's IQ did the things Koko does we'd call him – let's be frank now – stupid.

Well, in my experience I've seen some human Kokos in the casinos and they aren't just on the players' side of the casino equation. There are some casino decision-makers who would be intellectually challenged by Koko. Now, the overwhelming majority of casino-workers I've met go from pretty smart to damn smart, but a few languish in the Koko ranges – the lowland intellectual gorilla fields.

These casino Kokos often do a great disservice to their players, their employees and their industry, even though they have no awareness of this fact. They have instituted rules, regulations, and games that drive players away rather than bring players to them. In the interests of fairness, one must call a Koko a Koko if the name fits.

And I'm going to name names.

There is Jo...just kidding. I'm not naming names; even the Kokos have to eat. But what I will do now is name the policies that I think must have come from the Kokos of the casinos as these decisions are, to be generous, cuckoo or Kokonutty. Here goes:

Whoever first thought up the idea that in order to play two hands at blackjack you should have to play double the table minimum is a definite Koko. Really now, if the player wishes to play two hands, telling him he has to double his bet will often discourage him from doing so. The same player playing two hands makes just as much money for the casino as two players playing one hand each. It's the exact same thing! So why tell him he has to double his bet? It's stupid. Let him play two hands at the table minimum and the casino makes twice as much money. Ask him to double his bet and he might only bet one hand. Big players will play two hands with higher bets because they can afford to, so it won't discourage high-end two-hand play. Steve Wynn knew this and when he was in charge of the Mirage properties in Vegas he had the best blackjack games in the world – and the most crowded.

I just received word of truly ugly Kokonean experiences many craps players have had with a policy devised at a casino. As many of you know, there is a dice revolution slowly growing in the country and an increase in craps play (and casino hold is up a lot recently) because of it. This revolution has to do with the ability of some players to control the dice and the wishing and hoping of other players – and the *delusion* of other players – that they can do this too. It means setting the dice and taking care with your throw, regardless of whether you actually have the skill or not. However, some casinos have decided to create a whole new host of rules for careful shooters one of which is telling them that their arms cannot cross the C&E line when they throw.

This new Kokonut rule is intended to discourage careful shooters but all it really does is aggravate *all* craps players who leave these casinos and flock to other casinos (who welcome them with open arms and vaults) to avoid the tongue lashings that are purportedly regularly administered by the box people, floor people, pit people and any other Koko who happens to be swinging by. Indeed, it has gotten to a point where two players have written to me to tell me that the stick person (two *different* stick people mind you) hit their hands with the stick when their swings went over the Forbidden Zone! I thought corporal punishment was outlawed?

Another player wrote me to tell me that a stick person put his stick parallel to the layout and told the player his arm couldn't hit the stick which was protecting the Forbidden Zone. Recall what the Forbidden Zone was in the original movie *Planet of the Apes*, which was, strangely enough, also protected by sticks. It was the area destroyed by the humans and thus uninhabitable. That will be these casinos' craps games if these new "rules" continue. [One of the two players, a doctor, who was hit with the stick, was going to sue but I convinced him that it wouldn't look good in the papers for him to be involved in such a case. Instead, he has taken his substantial business elsewhere.] You can read about controlled shooting in Dominator's and my new book, *Golden Touch Dice Control Revolution!*

A truly Kokonesque moment occurred some years ago in Vegas when a casino proudly announced on a giant billboard that it was offering a single-deck blackjack game where a natural paid $6 to $5. Of course, a natural would usually pay $7.50 for $5 so this casino was trumpeting the fact that they were *screwing* the players big time. Just about then, many Strip casinos went to continuous automatic shufflers on their blackjack games to increase the number of hands a player played by 20 percent. And all the Strip casinos went to hitting Soft 17 to increase profits at blackjack as well. And in the years since these "profit-enhancing" rules went into effect what has happened? Instead of an increase in blackjack profits, the Vegas casinos have lost blackjack revenue! That sound you hear are the Kokos who created these "improvements" slipping on banana peels!

Yes, there are Kokos in every industry and line of work. I'm sure many of you when you meet with your extended families can point out the Kokos in your clan. Still, a gorilla is a gorilla. They are fun to watch as they swing on a tree limb and pound their chests and uproot logs looking for succulent bugs. But do you really want them in positions of authority? Uhaheehgagump! (That's gorilla for "NO WAY!")

But there are as many casino-player Kokos too. They can teach us just how stupid we players can be. The real Koko was raised by humans and taught American Sign Language, so she can actually communicate. Her active vocabulary is about 500 words, and she never says things like what teenagers say, "Well, like, you know, like I said, like, I wasn't, like, going to do that, like why should I or that's Phat!"

For a gorilla, Koko seems pretty savvy.

However, in a position of authority, Koko just couldn't hack it because, while she may be smart in gorilla terms, she's no world-beater in human terms. You don't want someone with an 85 IQ flying planes, doing brain surgery or making decisions in the casinos – especially a gorilla. I don't want to be comped to a banana.

But to be fair to casino executives, there are plenty of Koko players in the casinos and they are far more *visible* as they swing from machine to machine, game to game, causing havoc to their bankrolls and anyone who happens to make a decision at blackjack that is actually correct!

So this chapter is dedicated to that breed of gorilla who makes gaming unpleasant not only for himself but for thee, me, and the dealers as well. Every quote coming up I have heard with my own ears, every event I've seen with my own eyes.

At blackjack, the Koko is convinced he knows what's best for the table and does not hesitate to give you advice. "Never hit a 16 against a dealer's seven," he scolds as you look at your hand of 16 and see the dealer's 7 staring you in the face. In his own game, he has such peculiar moves as splitting tens, not splitting aces or eights against a dealer's 9, 10 or ace. And when you attempt to so split against said hands, he'll gently chide you with, "What're ya stoop-pid?"

The Koko is convinced that the dealer has a 10-valued card under every up card, even though the 10-valued cards make up a mere 31 percent of the shoe! If you make a move he doesn't like, and you happen to lose, God help you; he'll jump on it. "See, see, what'd I tell ya?" Should a 10-valued card actually be under the up card, you won't hear the end of it: "The dealer *always* has a ten in the hole!"

At craps the Koko continually presses his bets, before he ever takes down a win, because he's always looking for the monster roll, the hot hand which comes about once a week or so when random rollers shoot, and he always wants to make a killing, not just a profit. And when he loses his thrice-pressed bets to a seven-out, he moans and complains about all the rotten shooters. "Can't anyone shoot the dice?" Of course, when *he* shoots, it's a different story; he tries to pretend he doesn't care whether he wins or loses. He just flings the dice indifferently towards the other end of the table. It's almost as if he wishes to seven-out so he can go back to bitching and moaning about everyone else.

The Koko at roulette will cover every number; every single number, figuring he has to win on each and every spin. He doesn't realize that the house only pays 35 units on a win but he loses 37 units at the same time.

The Koko at a slot machine is a marvel to behold as he yells and hits the machine. "This damn thing is cold, ice cold," he complains as he puts in another hundred-dollar bill into the bill acceptor. If asked why he doesn't just abandon the machine and look for greener pastures elsewhere, he states confidently: "Because this machine is *due* to hit!"

The Koko has an annoying habit at the machines. If someone else is winning, he goes over to that person and hovers around them, hoping they will leave the machine and that he'll be able to take it over. "That's how I get on hot machines," he says confidentially, pulling out his ATM card to take yet another advance.

The Koko blames everyone and everything for his losses, everything that is but himself and his poor strategies. At blackjack, the third baseman caused him to lose because of the way the third baseman played his cards. At craps, the shooters stink. At roulette, the wheel is "off." At slots the machines are jinxed!

The Koko's most irritating trait is the fact that he thinks everyone gives two flying cents about *his* luck! He thinks he is the center of the gambling universe. Everyone should applaud his good luck; while his bad luck should bring on the sympathy from everyone. Unlike Job from the Bible, the player Koko enjoys the attention even horrendous luck brings him because that places him where he wants to be – in *your* face.

When he asks for a comp that is outrageously above his betting levels and playing time, he rails when the pit boss offers him the buffet instead. "I should get the steak house, at the very least!" he'll scream, when what he really deserves is "a trough of baked beans garnished with a couple of dead dogs" (I got that line from the great Brit-com *Fawlty Towers*).

The Koko makes casino gambling an unpleasant experience for the rest of us because his fate and face are always intruding on our space. He isn't just interested in what he's doing; he wants to make sure you are doing that too.

The Koko knows everything there is to know about gambling, politics, religion, philosophy, medicine, computers, love, and relationships. He can read the future, "I knew that was gonna happen!" And he knows the past, "This *always* happens!"

So what is the typical human player to do when confronted with a Koko at the tables; or when sitting next to a Koko at the machines? Get up and swing over to someplace where he isn't.

So what is the difference between a Ploppy and a Koko? Nothing really. Both are names to call people who annoy us.

Okay, your break is over. Back to the learning process.

- Chapter 6 -
Optimum Basic Strategy

7-7-7

If you got three 7s strung across the line of one of those slot machines the majority of the casino patrons play, you would be jumping up and down because you just received some very good news – you won a lot of money. Okay, this chapter requires little or no work but it is a gift, given you by our resident brainiac Dan Pronovost that acts kind of like those three 7s on a slot machine. You are getting a nice reward for no work at all.

Dan has come up with a new basic strategy that can be played only with Speed Count that enhances your edge at the game and also gives you built-in camouflage to throw the pit off to the fact that you are a highly skilled player. We call this new strategy OBS (Optimum Basic Strategy) and it is subtly different for different games. You can buy laminated, pocketsize Optimum Basic Strategy cards (see page 161). If you use the card, you don't even have to memorize the changes from the traditional basic strategy to play perfectly.

For those who thought Basic Strategy (BS) was the bible cast in stone, the mere suggestion of variations may seem like heresy. How can you make more money by playing differently when BS already has been optimized? Well, it turns out there is a big difference between optimizing your fixed playing strategy as a card counter and as a non-counter. And OBS is exactly that, a fixed playing strategy slightly different from traditional BS that is tuned to give you a better edge as a Speed Counter. Consider it the *New Testament* for blackjack.

When most card counters learn their craft, they spend a lot of time memorizing changes in the basic strategy based on the count to enhance their edge. These are called index plays, and they are notoriously difficult to master for most average counters as they tend to introduce errors in your play. Dan has made having to change strategies in mid-stream unnecessary because the OBS is based on what the best play of each hand is all the time, as a Speed Counter. You will note some unusual plays in the OBS but because you are using Speed Count these plays will make you more money than the traditional basic strategy. Again, Golden Touch Blackjack positions you to look like a regular player – and a somewhat dim one at that.

What follows is the OBS for all types of games. After the strategy, I discuss what the changes are from the traditional basic strategy to our new and improved OBS. The entries followed by a star (*) are different from the commonly accepted basic strategy.

If you've never seen a basic strategy table, then let me show you how easy it is to read it. The first OBS Table is to be used when you play blackjack at a table that uses anywhere from 2 to 8 decks of cards with these rules: dealer hits soft 17 (h17) and players are *not* allowed to double down after splitting a pair (noDAS). The first row is the dealer's upcard. The first column corresponds to your hand. At the intersection of a column and row you will see a letter like H. That letter represents the optimum playing strategy for that hand. For example, supposed you were dealt a 7-6 and the dealer's upcard is a 6. If you go down the first column to 13 and across that row to the column with the heading 6 (dealer's upcard) you see an S which means you should stand with 13 when the dealer shows a 6 upcard. At the bottom of the table is a glossary that explains what each letter means (H=Hit, S=Stand, etc.). Some of the blocks in the table have two letters separated by a forward slash (e.g., U/H). What this means is follow the strategy before the forward slash but if the rules do not allow you to do so, then use the strategy that follows the forward slash (e.g, U/H means surrender, but if the casinos don't allow surrender, then hit). In all the OBS Tables that follow, it is implied that the letter D means double down, but if the rules don't allow you to double down, then Hit. See, I told you this was easy.

Notice that the first column in the table labeled "Hand" contains three groupings of player hands. The first group consists of the hard hands from 8 through 16. The next group consists of the soft hands from Ace-2 through Ace-9 followed by the pairs (2-2 through T-T).

If you have a soft hand with 3 or more cards, this is how you would use the OBS Table. Suppose you are dealt Ace-3-4 or soft 18. You would look at the row beginning with A7 (soft 18) to determine how to play this hand. Similarly, if you had an Ace-2-2 hand, you would look at the A5 row for the correct playing decisions.

The hard 13 through 16 hands may also consist of 3 or more cards. For example, if you were dealt 3-4-6 you would look at the row beginning with 13 for the correct play decisions for this hand.

Sometimes a hand may begin as a soft hand and after drawing a card, convert to a hard hand. For example, suppose you were dealt an Ace-3 against a dealer's upcard of 7. The OBS Table states to hit. Suppose you draw a 9. Your hand converts to hard 13 (Ace-3-9). To determine how to proceed with the hand, you would have to look at the row beginning with 13 (or hard 13) and against the dealer's 7, the Table states to hit.

The OBS Tables do not have any entry for hands that total less than hard 8 or more than hard 16. However, you should always hit the former hands and stand on the latter using Speed Count.

With a little practice you should be able to use the OBS Table to determine how to play any hand dealt to you. You may also bring a hand held OBS Strategy Card with you on the tables when you play. For details on purchasing the OBS cards see page 161.

2-8 deck, noDAS, H17

Hand	2	3	4	5	6	7	8	9	10	A
8	H	H	H	H	D*	H	H	H	H	H
9	D*	D	D	D	D	H	H	H	H	H
10	D	D	D	D	D	D	D	D	H	H
11	D	D	D	D	D	D	D	D	D	D*
12	H	S*	S	S	S	H	H	H	H	H
13	S	S	S	S	S	H	H	H	H	H
14	S	S	S	S	S	H	H	H	H	H
15	S	S	S	S	S	H	H	H	U/H	U/H*
16	S	S	S	S	S	H	H	U/H	U/S*	U/H
A2	H	H	H	D	D	H	H	H	H	H
A3	H	H	D*	D	D	H	H	H	H	H
A4	H	H	D	D	D	H	H	H	H	H
A5	H	H	D	D	D	H	H	H	H	H
A6	H	D	D	D	D	H	H	H	H	H
A7	D/S*	D/S	D/S	D/S	D/S	S	S	H	H	H
A8	S	S	S	S	D/S*	S	S	S	S	S
A9	S	S	S	S	S	S	S	S	S	S
AA	P	P	P	P	P	P	P	P	P	P
22	H	H	P	P	P	P	H	H	H	H
33	H	H	P	P	P	P	H	H	H	H
44	H	H	H	H	D*	H	H	H	H	H
55	D	D	D	D	D	D	D	D	H	H
66	P*	P	P	P	P	H	H	H	H	H
77	P	P	P	P	P	P	H	H	U/H*	U/H*
88	P	P	P	P	P	P	P	P	U/P*	U/P*
99	P	P	P	P	P	S	P	P	S	S
TT	S	S	S	S	S	S	S	S	S	S

U=Surrender
D=Double
S=Stand
P=Split
H=Hit

- X/Y: if 'X' not possible, do 'Y'
- D: double if possible, else hit

2-8 deck, DAS, H17

Hand	2	3	4	5	6	7	8	9	10	A
8	H	H	H	H	D*	H	H	H	H	H
9	D*	D	D	D	D	H	H	H	H	H
10	D	D	D	D	D	D	D	D	H	H
11	D	D	D	D	D	D	D	D	D	D*
12	H	S*	S	S	S	H	H	H	H	H
13	S	S	S	S	S	H	H	H	H	H
14	S	S	S	S	S	H	H	H	H	H
15	S	S	S	S	S	H	H	H	U/H	U/H*
16	S	S	S	S	S	H	H	U/H	U/S*	U/H
A2	H	H	H	D	D	H	H	H	H	H
A3	H	H	D*	D	D	H	H	H	H	H
A4	H	H	D	D	D	H	H	H	H	H
A5	H	H	D	D	D	H	H	H	H	H
A6	H	D	D	D	D	H	H	H	H	H
A7	D/S*	D/S	D/S	D/S	D/S	S	S	H	H	H
A8	S	S	S	S	D/S*	S	S	S	S	S
A9	S	S	S	S	S	S	S	S	S	S
AA	P	P	P	P	P	P	P	P	P	P
22	P	P	P	P	P	P	H	H	H	H
33	P	P	P	P	P	P	H	H	H	H
44	H	H	H	P	P	H	H	H	H	H
55	D	D	D	D	D	D	D	D	H	H
66	P	P	P	P	P	H	H	H	H	H
77	P	P	P	P	P	P	P*	H	U/H*	U/H*
88	P	P	P	P	P	P	P	P	U/P*	U/P*
99	P	P	P	P	P	S	P	P	S	S
TT	S	S	S	S	S	S	S	S	S	S

U=Surrender
D=Double
S=Stand
P=Split
H=Hit

- X/Y: if 'X' not possible, do 'Y'
- D: double if possible, else hit

2-8 deck, DAS, S17

Hand	2	3	4	5	6	7	8	9	10	A
8	H	H	H	H	D*	H	H	H	H	H
9	D*	D	D	D	D	H	H	H	H	H
10	D	D	D	D	D	D	D	D	H	H
11	D	D	D	D	D	D	D	D	D	D*
12	H	S*	S	S	S	H	H	H	H	H
13	S	S	S	S	S	H	H	H	H	H
14	S	S	S	S	S	H	H	H	H	H
15	S	S	S	S	S	H	H	H	U/H	U/H*
16	S	S	S	S	S	H	H	U/H	U/S*	U/H
A2	H	H	H	D	D	H	H	H	H	H
A3	H	H	D*	D	D	H	H	H	H	H
A4	H	H	D	D	D	H	H	H	H	H
A5	H	H	D	D	D	H	H	H	H	H
A6	H	D	D	D	D	H	H	H	H	H
A7	D/S*	D/S	D/S	D/S	D/S	S	S	H	H	S*
A8	S	S	S	S	D/S*	S	S	S	S	S
A9	S	S	S	S	S	S	S	S	S	S
AA	P	P	P	P	P	P	P	P	P	P
22	P	P	P	P	P	P	H	H	H	H
33	P	P	P	P	P	P	H	H	H	H
44	H	H	H	P	P	H	H	H	H	H
55	D	D	D	D	D	D	D	D	H	H
66	P	P	P	P	P	H	H	H	H	H
77	P	P	P	P	P	P	H	H	U/H*	U/H*
88	P	P	P	P	P	P	P	P	U/P*	P
99	P	P	P	P	P	S	P	P	S	S
TT	S	S	S	S	S	S	S	S	S	S

U=Surrender
D=Double
S=Stand
P=Split
H=Hit

- X/Y: if 'X' not possible, do 'Y'
- D: double if possible, else hit

2-8 deck, noDAS, S17

Hand	2	3	4	5	6	7	8	9	10	A
8	H	H	H	H	D*	H	H	H	H	H
9	D*	D	D	D	D	H	H	H	H	H
10	D	D	D	D	D	D	D	D	H	H
11	D	D	D	D	D	D	D	D	D	D*
12	H	S*	S	S	S	H	H	H	H	H
13	S	S	S	S	S	H	H	H	H	H
14	S	S	S	S	S	H	H	H	H	H
15	S	S	S	S	S	H	H	H	U/H	U/H*
16	S	S	S	S	S	H	H	U/H	U/S*	U/H
A2	H	H	H	D	D	H	H	H	H	H
A3	H	H	D*	D	D	H	H	H	H	H
A4	H	H	D	D	D	H	H	H	H	H
A5	H	H	D	D	D	H	H	H	H	H
A6	H	D	D	D	D	H	H	H	H	H
A7	D/S*	D/S	D/S	D/S	D/S	S	S	H	H	S*
A8	S	S	S	S	D/S*	S	S	S	S	S
A9	S	S	S	S	S	S	S	S	S	S
AA	P	P	P	P	P	P	P	P	P	P
22	H	H	P	P	P	P	H	H	H	H
33	H	H	P	P	P	P	H	H	H	H
44	H	H	H	H	D*	H	H	H	H	H
55	D	D	D	D	D	D	D	D	H	H
66	P*	P	P	P	P	H	H	H	H	H
77	P	P	P	P	P	P	H	H	U/H*	U/H*
88	P	P	P	P	P	P	P	P	U/P*	P
99	P	P	P	P	P	S	P	P	S	S
TT	S	S	S	S	S	S	S	S	S	S

U=Surrender
D=Double
S=Stand
P=Split
H=Hit

- X/Y: if 'X' not possible, do 'Y'
- D: double if possible, else hit

Single deck, noDAS, H17

Hand	2	3	4	5	6	7	8	9	10	A
8	H	H	H	D	D	H	H	H	H	H
9	D	D	D	D	D	H	H	H	H	H
10	D	D	D	D	D	D	D	D	H	H
11	D	D	D	D	D	D	D	D	D	D
12	H	H	S	S	S	H	H	H	H	H
13	S	S	S	S	S	H	H	H	H	H
14	S	S	S	S	S	H	H	H	H	H
15	S	S	S	S	S	H	H	H	U/H*	U/H*
16	S	S	S	S	S	H	H	U/H*	U/H	U/H*
A2	H	H	D	D	D	H	H	H	H	H
A3	H	H	D	D	D	H	H	H	H	H
A4	H	H	D	D	D	H	H	H	H	H
A5	H	H	D	D	D	H	H	H	H	H
A6	D	D	D	D	D	H	H	H	H	H
A7	S	D/S	D/S	D/S	D/S	S	S	H	H	H
A8	S	S	S	D/S*	D/S	S	S	S	S	S
A9	S	S	S	S	S	S	S	S	S	S
AA	P	P	P	P	P	P	P	P	P	P
22	H	P	P	P	P	P	H	H	H	H
33	H	H	P	P	P	P	H	H	H	H
44	H	H	H	D	D	H	H	H	H	H
55	D	D	D	D	D	D	D	D	H	H
66	P	P	P	P	P	H	H	H	H	H
77	P	P	P	P	P	P	H	H	U/S	U/H*
88	P	P	P	P	P	P	P	P	P	P
99	P	P	P	P	P	S	P	P	S	P*
TT	S	S	S	S	S	S	S	S	S	S

U=Surrender
D=Double
S=Stand
P=Split
H=Hit

- X/Y: if 'X' not possible, do 'Y'
- D: double if possible, else hit

Single deck, DAS, H17

Hand	2	3	4	5	6	7	8	9	10	A
8	H	H	H	D	D	H	H	H	H	H
9	D	D	D	D	D	H	H	H	H	H
10	D	D	D	D	D	D	D	D	H	H
11	D	D	D	D	D	D	D	D	D	D
12	H	H	S	S	S	H	H	H	H	H
13	S	S	S	S	S	H	H	H	H	H
14	S	S	S	S	S	H	H	H	H	H
15	S	S	S	S	S	H	H	H	U/H*	U/H*
16	S	S	S	S	S	H	H	U/H*	U/H	U/H*
A2	H	H	D	D	D	H	H	H	H	H
A3	H	H	D	D	D	H	H	H	H	H
A4	H	H	D	D	D	H	H	H	H	H
A5	H	H	D	D	D	H	H	H	H	H
A6	D	D	D	D	D	H	H	H	H	H
A7	S	D/S	D/S	D/S	D/S	S	S	H	H	H
A8	S	S	S	D/S*	D/S	S	S	S	S	S
A9	S	S	S	S	S	S	S	S	S	S
AA	P	P	P	P	P	P	P	P	P	P
22	P	P	P	P	P	P	H	H	H	H
33	P	P	P	P	P	P	H	H	H	H
44	H	H	P	P	P	H	H	H	H	H
55	D	D	D	D	D	D	D	D	H	H
66	P	P	P	P	P	P	H	H	H	H
77	P	P	P	P	P	P	P	H	U/S	U/H*
88	P	P	P	P	P	P	P	P	P	P
99	P	P	P	P	P	S	P	P	S	P*
TT	S	S	S	S	S	S	S	S	S	S

U=Surrender
D=Double
S=Stand
P=Split
H=Hit

- X/Y: if 'X' not possible, do 'Y'
- D: double if possible, else hit

Single deck, DAS,S17

Hand	2	3	4	5	6	7	8	9	10	A
8	H	H	H	D	D	H	H	H	H	H
9	D	D	D	D	D	H	H	H	H	H
10	D	D	D	D	D	D	D	D	H	H
11	D	D	D	D	D	D	D	D	D	D
12	H	H	S	S	S	H	H	H	H	H
13	S	S	S	S	S	H	H	H	H	H
14	S	S	S	S	S	H	H	H	H	H
15	S	S	S	S	S	H	H	H	U/H*	U/H*
16	S	S	S	S	S	H	H	U/H*	U/H	U/H*
A2	H	H	D	D	D	H	H	H	H	H
A3	H	H	D	D	D	H	H	H	H	H
A4	H	H	D	D	D	H	H	H	H	H
A5	H	H	D	D	D	H	H	H	H	H
A6	D	D	D	D	D	H	H	H	H	H
A7	S	D/S	D/S	D/S	D/S	S	S	H	H	S
A8	S	S	S	D/S*	D/S	S	S	S	S	S
A9	S	S	S	S	S	S	S	S	S	S
AA	P	P	P	P	P	P	P	P	P	P
22	P	P	P	P	P	P	H	H	H	H
33	P	P	P	P	P	P	H	H	H	H
44	H	H	P	P	P	H	H	H	H	H
55	D	D	D	D	D	D	D	D	H	H
66	P	P	P	P	P	P	H	H	H	H
77	P	P	P	P	P	P	P	H	U/S	U/H*
88	P	P	P	P	P	P	P	P	P	P
99	P	P	P	P	P	S	P	P	S	S
TT	S	S	S	S	S	S	S	S	S	S

U=Surrender
D=Double
S=Stand
P=Split
H=Hit

- X/Y: if 'X' not possible, do 'Y'
- D: double if possible, else hit

Single deck, noDAS, S17

Hand	2	3	4	5	6	7	8	9	10	A
8	H	H	H	D	D	H	H	H	H	H
9	D	D	D	D	D	H	H	H	H	H
10	D	D	D	D	D	D	D	D	H	H
11	D	D	D	D	D	D	D	D	D	D
12	H	H	S	S	S	H	H	H	H	H
13	S	S	S	S	S	H	H	H	H	H
14	S	S	S	S	S	H	H	H	H	H
15	S	S	S	S	S	H	H	H	U/H*	U/H*
16	S	S	S	S	S	H	H	U/H*	U/H	U/H*
A2	H	H	D	D	D	H	H	H	H	H
A3	H	H	D	D	D	H	H	H	H	H
A4	H	H	D	D	D	H	H	H	H	H
A5	H	H	D	D	D	H	H	H	H	H
A6	D	D	D	D	D	H	H	H	H	H
A7	S	D/S	D/S	D/S	D/S	S	S	H	H	S
A8	S	S	S	D/S*	D/S	S	S	S	S	S
A9	S	S	S	S	S	S	S	S	S	S
AA	P	P	P	P	P	P	P	P	P	P
22	H	P	P	P	P	P	H	H	H	H
33	H	H	P	P	P	P	H	H	H	H
44	H	H	H	D	D	H	H	H	H	H
55	D	D	D	D	D	D	D	D	H	H
66	P	P	P	P	P	H	H	H	H	H
77	P	P	P	P	P	P	H	H	U/S	U/H*
88	P	P	P	P	P	P	P	P	P	P
99	P	P	P	P	P	S	P	P	S	S
TT	S	S	S	S	S	S	S	S	S	S

U=Surrender
D=Double
S=Stand
P=Split
H=Hit

- X/Y: if 'X' not possible, do 'Y'
- D: double if possible, else hit

Modifications in OBS

Now is the time that some math gurus are going to pour over the previous tables and declare that some play we've recommended is not optimal in some particular game. And our answer is, "Yup... we simplified the previous tables a little in ways that have insignificant impact on your earning potential." Actually Dominator said this, "Hey, math guru, if you are such a big shot traditional card counter why are you reading this book? And who cares what you have to say since you are so advanced? Bug off!"

How did we simplify?

For starters, we only considered the four combinations of DAS/noDAS, and H17/S17. Also, we lumped the games into two categories: single-deck, and everything else. This makes for 8 tables in total. We also assumed average penetrations for the respective games (50 percent for single-deck, 66.67 percent for double-deck, and 75 percent for four or more decks), and only looked at games with six players and also with one player, which is head-to-head against the dealer.

The next thing Dan did was run an incredibly large number of simulations with his software using different strategies for different games with Speed Count. In most cases, one single strategy variation dominated as the better play and was selected. In the small number of cases where more than one strategy may be optimal based on the same factor, Dan made sure the difference was negligible and not worth the extra learning hassle. Luckily, this turned out to be true, but it did mean we had to create a unique strategy set for single-deck. Dan had hoped to 'unify' it too, but single-deck really is a different animal.

We placed stars in the above tables where you might find differences from traditional basic strategy. Now, you might notice some cases that are odd to you. Most people think that there can be only one optimal blackjack strategy for any given play, and get quite self-righteous when they see two different recommended plays. But the reality is that some cases are borderline, and two completely different strategies can make little difference to your edge. More importantly, it may make more sense to choose your play based on a different factor (such as simplifying or coalescing the tables) rather than nitpicking over a four decimal place difference in edge! The important thing is that Dan spent the time for you analyzing this to death, to find the balance between performance and ease of memorization. Our OBS will give you the best edge with Speed Count in all the games listed.

How much of a difference does OBS make when compared to traditional basic strategy? From the table on page 136, we can see that a six-deck DAS/S17 game played heads up against the dealer with Speed Count Conservative yields a positive edge of 0.4209 percent (using OBS, of course). If we instead use traditional basic strategy (see the starred items in the corresponding table earlier in this chapter), your edge worsens to 0.3685 percent, a performance drop of 12 percent, which is significant. Depending on the game and basic strategy you are comparing against, you can expect to generally see about a 10 percent boost in performance by using OBS. And that, my dear readers, means more money in your pocket in the long run when you use the OBS.

- Chapter 7 -
Bankroll and Risk of Ruin (ROR)

I mentioned this before but it is good to mention it again. You can lose. You can have a losing session today. You can have several losing sessions in a row – today, tonight, and all day tomorrow. You can have a losing trip. You can have many losing trips – even in a row. The fact that you have an edge does not guarantee that each and every time you step up to the blackjack table you are going to win. Having an edge means that in the long run you will come out ahead. In the short run, your head can be handed to you.

What prevents astute advantage players from going nuts when they hit those inevitable losing streaks is the fact that they have an *adequate bankroll* to sustain them while Lady Luck flogs them unmercifully. They also have what I call a strong *emotional bankroll* that allows them to take the losses in stride. You must have both a real and *sufficient* monetary bankroll and also a strong emotional bankroll to survive the fluctuations that you will experience when you play advantage blackjack. Trust me on this.

If you are under financed, you can have your bankroll wiped out. That's right, even with an edge a bad streak can come along that wipes you out. You must have plenty of money behind you to be able to withstand the losing streaks.

Let me give you a simple but powerful example of what I am talking about. Let us say you want to engage your nephew, Little Timmy, in a game of flip the coin. Each flip is for a dollar. If you win, you win a dollar. However, we want to give Little Timmy a giant edge over you, so every time he wins, he receives a dollar and 10 cents. Wow! Your bankroll for this contest is one million dollars. His bankroll is two dollars. He has a very large mathematical edge over you. He is also doomed to lose. The first sustained losing streak is going to put Little Timmy away. He just doesn't have the bankroll to engage in the contest with you. He could lose the first two tosses and he's a dead man, er, kid.

The same is true of a Golden Toucher or any advantage player at blackjack. You have to have the edge *plus* a sufficient bankroll to win. That's the bottom line of winning play.

The mathematicians call having a sufficient bankroll a part of their Risk of Ruin (ROR) formula. Risk of Ruin is just that. Given "X" amount of money and betting this particular spread at a particular game, what are the chances that I will wind up like Little Timmy – dead broke and crying my eyes out? If I want to bet $10 to $40 using Speed Count in a double-deck game, how much will I need in my bankroll for 100 hands, for 200 hands, for 2,000 hands, for 20,000 hands and for two million hands in order to insure me that I have a 95 percent chance to last at the game no matter how fickle Lady Luck gets?

I have to tell you a little story about my blackjack-playing career to give you a sense of how awful losing one's entire gambling stake can be. The mathematicians say "risk of ruin" and that is a clean way of really saying, "I got my ass kicked hard!" Here's my story:

When my wife, the beautiful A.P., and I gave up theatre for the joys of challenging the casinos using advantage play, we put aside $5,000 as our bankroll. This was in the 1980s. We worked on our High-Low card counting and I memorized four zillion strategy changes from basic strategy based on the count (these changes are called indices by the blackjack cognoscenti). We then went to Atlantic City, the Queen of Resorts.

In those glorious days of the 1980s, Atlantic City was not a 24/7 town. It was a 20/7 or an 18/7 town or something like that. It also had some wonderful, deeply penetrated four-deck games with late surrender, great rules and non-paranoid pit bosses (if you were betting red and small green action, which we were). My bet spread was 1 to 8 on the four-deck games, enough to give me a healthy edge. In dollars, this means I was spreading from $10 to $80.

We stayed in Atlantic City for nine days and absolutely destroyed them. I don't think we lost a single playing session. We'd play about eight or nine hours a day and I really thought to myself, "I am going to become a billionaire! This card counting is so easy and profitable. You know I might even buy myself a casino."

When we came home I decided to schedule another trip right away. This time we went for 16 days. The worst 16 days of my blackjack-playing life. We lost and lost and lost. I started to bet bigger than I had planned in high counts, counts which heavily favored me – and I lost. I would wait for the casinos to open in the morning and be the first at the tables. And lost. I played all day long. I played most of the night.

And lost.

I lost all the money we had won on our last trip and all the money we had saved to be professional gamblers. While I was not broke in my real life, I had lost all the money I had set aside for my gambling life. On the way back home we stopped off at the Captain's house (the Captain is my gambling mentor and the subject of many of my books) where he gave A.P. and me a lesson about gambling and human rhythm that we have never forgotten. He also taught us about bankroll requirements.

I was under financed in those days – or I was betting too big for the money I did have. I was also out of my mind because I thought, "Things have to change! Things have to get better! I will bet more and get all my money back!" Yes, I was dumb. Despite having an edge over the house, I lost my very first gambling bankroll – every single penny of it.

You'll note that while I was a partner with the beautiful A.P., I can't put any of the blame for the loss on her. She wanted to play conservatively. She wanted our bets to be based on sound principles. She wanted to play relaxed, normal-length sessions. I was the one who had lost his cool and our cash.

Today, I have another bankroll, one that I will never be able to lose in the casinos because I no longer play like a fool and bet like a madman in relation to that bankroll. I discovered in those heady days of the 1980s that losing my money emotionally hurts me more than winning money makes me happy. The negative is stronger than the positive for me. Knowing this, I have given myself a strict rule – I have a virtually zero risk of ruin for my bankroll. Zero. Zip. Aught. Cipher. Duck egg. Goose egg. Nada. Nadir. Naught. Nil. Nought. Zilch. Zot. That of course means I squirrel away a huge bankroll to play with, but it also means I no longer sweat the ups and downs like I used to.

And that makes me feel good. That allows me to play perfectly.

Now many card counters, when they hear me say this, think, "The guy is an idiot! He's betting too small for his bankroll if he has such a low Risk of Ruin." Maybe so. But I never have to worry that I will be wiped out no matter how bad the current bad streak becomes. I need that kind of bankroll to allow me to have the *emotional bankroll* to play these casino games fearlessly – otherwise they aren't worth playing. I hate to lose money more than I like to win money. Period.

Dan has great tables in the Appendix for all sorts of Risk of Ruin scenarios (see page 142). We will peg all of them at 5 percent, which means you will have a 5 percent chance to lose the entire bankroll being analyzed in the charts. Let me show you one example now – so you get a good feel for how to handle the risk of ruin calculations that Dan will give you.

Let us say that you are playing a double-deck game, S17, DAS and you want to play for four hours in a given day. You are a $10 bettor and you will spread one to four units using Conservative Speed Count. In order to give you a 5 percent Risk of Ruin – which means a 5 percent chance of losing every penny in your session stake – you must have $1,044 for that day of play. If you have less, your chances of busting out increase. If you were to give yourself an $890 bankroll for the day, your chance of losing it all zooms up to 10 percent. Yes, that means 10 percent of the time with a day's bankroll of $890; you will lose it all even though in the long run you will make money with Speed Count.

In order to make sure that you have enough money behind you, you need to look at three types of bankrolls:

1. Session bankrolls

2. Trip bankrolls

3. Total bankroll

Obviously the most important bankroll is number three. How much money have you put aside for your long-term advantage play at blackjack? Your total bankroll dictates what your betting level will be given the Risk of Ruin that you can tolerate. The trip bankroll is how much of your bankroll you will bring with you on your trips to the casinos and your session bankroll is how much bankroll you will give yourself to play a given session or day.

If you were playing the two-deck game above, your lifetime Risk of Ruin at 5 percent would necessitate a total bankroll of approximately $10,225. Personally, a 5 percent total Risk of Ruin is way too much for me. I want fractions of a percent!

Of course, you will win more money than you lose over time, and your bankroll will ultimately go up. If you are comfortable with a 5 percent Risk of Ruin, you can increase your betting levels as your bankroll increases. Or, you can first reduce the percent of your Risk of Ruin by allowing your bankroll to grow without increasing your bet size. When you get to a one percent or half percent or quarter percent Risk of Ruin, you can then increase your bets accordingly. You have to decide how you want to proceed. Some of what you will do will not be based on math but on your emotional ability to bet certain amounts knowing that you can lose.

How do you know you are betting too much money? When you lose you think of other things you could have done with the money. "Gee," you think, "I could have had that heart surgery I need." If that happens, then you must reduce what you are wagering. Otherwise you might just have that heart attack due to the stress of wagering.

Here is another example of how Risk of Ruin could wreak havoc in the short term with a Speed Count player. The Speed Counter plans to bring $1,000 and play about 8 hours of blackjack over a weekend in Atlantic City using a $10 to $80 bet spread. But when he arrives the casino is packed with players at all times and the only open seat he can find is at a $15 minimum table. So he sits down and plays anyway. Big mistake. Why? His Risk of Ruin spreading $15 to $120 is 50 percent! That means half of the time he will lose $1,000 over a weekend even though he has the long term positive edge using Speed Count. Listen to what I and Dan and Henry and Dominator implore you: always keep your Risk of Ruin to 5 percent (or less) by not over-betting in relation to your bankroll. OK?

How did we come up with all these glorious bankroll numbers and calculations? We turned to resident math geek Dan of course, who in turn used his *Blackjack Audit* simulation software. You can compute both trip and lifetime risk of ruin for any blackjack game, using either the calculators in his software or his nifty Risk of Ruin simulators. See page 115 for more details on the Speed Count software.

The 401-G

If you want to be a serious advantage player, my recommendation to you is to start a 401-G. A 401-G is a money-market checking account that you use for your gambling dollars. You should never be using "real" money when you play in the casinos; you should only be using money that you have set aside specifically for playing. This 401-G (the "G" stands for gambling) can go a long way towards strengthening your emotional bankroll too. Knowing you have the proper amount of money in a single account to play at the level you feel comfortable with will, well, make you feel even more comfortable.

As you win money, you put it in your 401-G; when you lose money, you lose it from your 401-G. Now what should you do if you lose, say, 20 percent of your total bankroll in a horrendous series of defeats? A smart move would be to reduce your total bet spread by 20 percent so that your Risk of Ruin stays at 5 percent or whatever level you feel comfortable with. If you win and increase your 401-G by 20 percent, you can increase your betting by this percentage as well. If you follow this advice, over time your 401-G will increase.

- Chapter 8 -
The Casinos Hate Card Counters

86ed

Speed Count will give you the edge at the game of blackjack. You will win money in the long run. And the more you play the better it is for you. We like that. I am sure you like that fact too. Speed Count is easy to learn and easy to use. It is a wonderful thing to be able to get the edge over the casino Goliath, isn't it? You are a little David and the casinos are these big monsters – and you can beat them with your little Golden Touch slingshot.

Of course, the casinos will hate you if they learn you can beat them. You understand that, right? Advantage players are the scum of the earth to the casino bosses. One boss recently called them "earners" with total disdain in his voice. Yes, they "earn" money because they can beat the casino games. In fact, they are smart. The casinos hate smart. Smart is bad.

The stories of card counters being back roomed, beaten, harassed, thrown out of their hotel rooms in the middle of the night are not fictions invented by the propeller hats. In the past (mostly) awful things were done to law-abiding citizens by the casino executives and security forces obsessed with protecting their games from advantage players who were not doing anything illegal.

The same smiling casino executive photographed with that smiling slot patron who has just won a million dollars on a machine will be the same guy snarling, foaming, sputtering and spewing to a card counter whose expectation is twenty bucks an hour, "We don't want you here, you are too good for us." This same executive will tell bigger players, "I am reading you the trespass act and if you show up here again we will arrest you for trespassing."

Yes, it's like being in high school again. The smart kids are hated; the dumb ones rule. Smart is bad. Dumb is good. The casinos are Ploppy heaven.

Card counters and other advantage players are the bane of the casinos' existence. Yes, the casinos offer games for the public to play but when some members of the public figure out how to beat those games well, "Get your fat or skinny butt out of our casino!" scream the executives.

The casinos want losers. The casinos cater to losers. The casinos love losers.

The casinos hate winners. They hate earners. They hate smart.

If you learn the Golden Touch Blackjack strategy, you will be a winner. You will be an earner because you are smart.

Oh, yes, the casinos will boot policemen, firemen, teachers, doctors, nurses, military veterans, and Medal of Honor winners from their properties if these individuals can beat the games. Mother Theresa? Out! The casinos will boot those who have fought in our country's wars; those who ran into the World Trade Center to save the lives of their fellow citizens from the monstrous terrorism perpetrated there.

It doesn't matter who these citizens are, the response is the same: "Out! Out! Out! You are too good for our games!" The casino executives don't care that their fellow citizens are being singled out for using their brains to beat the casinos' games. Their response is "Out!"

It's a disgrace.

It's un-American.

It's Un-Canadian.

It's nauseating.

It's immoral.

It's also the truth, too.

You could be Jesus Christ or Moses or Buddha but if you can count cards and they figure it out, you won't be welcomed in the casinos. Go walk on water elsewhere! Go part the sea elsewhere! Do your eight fold path in someone else's garden! *Out! Out! Out!*

Unfortunately, the law is on the casinos' side for the most part. These casino businesses are not public enterprises – they are private entities and as such, they have the right to refuse service to anyone they want to. They can't discriminate because of your race, that's true, or your gender or religion or handicapping condition. But they can discriminate against your brain and your skill.

The casino executives have several ways of handling a threat to their profits.

They can "ask" you not to play blackjack, yes, but they also might say, "You can play any other game here," or, if they want, they can *tell* you to get lost and not come back to their property ever again. Casinos cannot, however, drag you into the back room and pummel the living daylights out of you (yes, in the past this has happened to some unfortunate card counters) and, in fact, if a casino stops you from playing and then "requests" that you come to the back room, you have the right to ask if they are calling the police. If they are, tell them you'll wait right where you are until the police arrive.

Since card counting is not illegal, you cannot be arrested for such intelligent use of your brain. If a casino tells you to beat it, then just beat it. Don't argue with the executive – he isn't interested in your opinions. Don't even talk to the executive. And don't show him your Medal of Honor. It won't change his mind. Just take your chips and leave. You can come back tomorrow and cash your chips in. Or you can send a friend to cash in your chips. Leave.

But…

Always be courteous. Never touch a casino employee in these situations as the casino might press assault charges against you. Don't yell and scream or they can have you arrested for being a disorderly person. Those grandly massively rock-solid muscled security people are very delicate at these times. Use your brain and just get out of the casino.

Now, will **you** have to really worry about being asked not to play? Probably not.

Henry, Dom, Dan and I have been playing blackjack for a long, long time and we've only experienced a few unpleasant moments with casino executives hungry to stop us from playing. If you use your head and don't give any casino sustained action hour after hour, it will be very hard for the pit to see that you are playing with an edge when you use our Golden Touch strategies. Yes, it is possible that you might get nailed (the more aggressively you bet the better your chances of this happening) and, if so, welcome to the club as all good card counters have occasionally been "asked" to stop playing.

The best recommendation we can make is to keep your sessions at no more than 45 minutes to an hour long. If you are a high roller or playing very aggressively, a half-hour session *and out* is a good way to go. It does take the casino some time to analyze your play and see that you have the edge over the game. If you are a rated player at the black-chip level, you should spread out your play on different shifts. Give the casino a moving target.

When you are playing the Golden Touch way, remember that you are doing many things no card counters do. You have built in camouflage protecting you because of these things.

1. You are sitting at first base (if possible).
2. You are not watching the cards as they are dealt.
3. You aren't interested in the sums of the hands of the other players or of the dealer.

4. Speed Count has you betting at a count of 31, which is a little earlier than most traditional systems that are more conservative, so it's less obvious.

You also have a camouflage element in the new basic strategy that we have given you. The Optimum Basic Strategy (OBS) is something that not only increases your edge with Speed Count but it also makes you look like a poor basic strategy player. Standing on 12 against a dealer's 3; standing on 16 versus a dealer's 10-card; doubling on your 8s; and doubling your Ace-8 at times will make you look pretty stupid to the floor person or pit boss.

Remember, in the casinos stupid is a synonym for *good*.

The Optimum Basic Strategy is a key element in the camouflage of Golden Touch Blackjack. It's a wonderful thing – increases your edge and makes you look dull.

Other Camouflage Techniques

Those of you who have read other blackjack books know that traditional card counters spend a lot of time figuring out ways to fool the pit into thinking they aren't card counters. As a Golden Touch blackjack player betting conservatively (or close to conservatively) we don't think you need to worry about camouflage since there is great built in camouflage with Speed Count and the OBS. Using other costly camouflage techniques might just make your small edge even smaller.

Aggressive players betting green, black and purple (plus) levels might want to follow some principles that gamblers use. You can mix and match these. Conservative bettors can use some of these as well – the ones that don't cost you money. (I have starred* the ones that cost you money.)

1. *When the count goes up, increase your bet if you have won the last hand. If you have lost the last hand do not increase your bet.

2. *If the count goes up and you lost only add a half unit, even if the proper bet is higher.

3. *If the count is high and you have a big bet up and the cut card comes out, do not lower your bet for the start of a new shoe.

4. Distribute your bets unevenly on two hands. Rarely do counters play two hands of unequal wagers.

5. Always be friendly to the pit. Casinos think that card counters tend to be somewhat standoffish.

6. You can talk about good or bad luck – but never mention skill.

7. Use an OBS card. Explain that you made it up to help you. When the pit looks at the OBS card they will see "mistakes." Good!

8. If you have hammered the casino in a high count and you have a nice profit, consider leaving and heading for another casino. A big win brings attention.

9. *If you push a hand with a big bet out and the count goes down, do not lower your bet. Gamblers usually keep the same units up following a push.

10. *If you push a hand and the count goes up, leave the same bet up. Gamblers rarely increase bets after pushes.

11. *Do not use play deviations from OBS to make you look stupid. You look stupid enough when using the OBS. Play variations cost you too much money.

12. Feel free to bitch and moan when you lose hands. That's normal behavior in the casinos.

13. Join in when your fellow players congratulate the third base player with his smart play that "saved the table."

12 *Things to Avoid at the Blackjack Tables*

There are some things you must never say or do at the blackjack tables. Here they are.

1. "What's the count?"

2. "Stop dealing so fast, I can't keep the count."

3. "Do you give good penetration?"

4. "...29, 30, 31, 33, 37 – Hooray! Time to bet big!"

5. Don't move your lips when you are adding up the small cards.

6. "I count cards so when I raise my bets all of you at the table should raise your bets too."

7. "Hey, stop spreading hands, it makes it hard to keep my count."

8. "I only take insurance in high counts."

9. "You won't throw me out because I'm counting cards, will you?"

10. "Hey everyone, Speed Count is so easy to use to get an edge at blackjack!"

11. "My real name is Ken Uston and I'm ready to play!"

12. "I am good friends with Frank Scoblete, Henry Tamburin, Dan Pronovost and Dominator! Deal the cards."

- Chapter 9 -
Blackjack Superstitions

All these blackjack superstitions are good to pretend to believe in when you are at the tables. It just makes you appear stupid, a thing we harp on. Stupid is good. Smart is bad. These superstitions are stupid. That is good – as long as you really don't believe them that is.

Bad players at the table will cause you to lose

The third baseman has a 16 and the dealer is showing a 6 as his up card. The third baseman decides to hit and gets a 10, busting him. The dealer turns over his hole card and he has a 10. The dealer now has 16. The dealer takes a hit and gets a 5, making his hand a 21.

Is the third baseman, who is obviously a poor player, responsible for your losing?

If you said "yes" you are wrong.

Take a look at the scenario. Suppose there are two cards that can come up next, a 5 or a 10, or a 10 and a 5. We don't know what order these two cards are in. If the third baseman decides to hit, there is a 50-50 chance he will get the 5 and the dealer will get the 10 or there is a 50-50 chance that the third baseman will get the 10 and the dealer will get the 5.

If the third baseman decides to stand, there is a 50-50 chance that the dealer will get the 5 and a 50-50 chance that the dealer will get the 10, busting him.

It's 50-50 no matter what the third baseman does.

A new player entering a game in the middle of the shoe screws up the order of the cards

Okay, go back to the example above. There are two cards that might come out, a 5 or a 10. Instead of the third baseman making a poor move, a new player entered the game just before this round was dealt. What card will the dealer get? If the new player can screw up the order of the cards should those two cards be changed in some way? But they aren't.

There is no order to the cards. You can't see the cards so you have no idea what order they are in. A new player might make the hands better or worse or not change anything at all – because a new player has no control over anything.

Those two cards are a 50-50 event at the end of the round. The dealer will either bust or he'll make it to 21.

Always stand on a soft hand like A-5 because if you hit, or double, it will get worse

Continuing with the above scenario. You are now at third base. The dealer is still showing his 6. You can take a hit or double down (doubling is the right move). The two cards to come out are still a 5 and a 10, but we don't know what order they are in. Will doubling help or hurt you?

It's a 50-50 proposition again.

If you double (or hit), you can get the 10. You would stand on your 16 against the dealer's 6. The dealer will hit his 16, get the 5 and you lose. Or, you double; you get the 5, and make it to 21. The dealer hits his 16, gets a 10 and busts. You win.

Let us say, you do nothing. You stand with you're A-5. What then? It's still 50-50. The dealer will beat you half the time and half the time the dealer will bust.

Picture cards always follow picture cards. If you've just seen a picture card, don't hit your stiff hand

In a deck of 52 cards, 16 of them are picture cards (we count the 10 here) so that is 31 percent of the deck. If you have seen two picture cards, the percent of tens in the deck is now down to 28 percent. Hitting a stiff hand (12, 13, 14, 15, and 16) is now a better proposition for you.

This superstition is harmful to you if you follow it.

Never hit a 12, because you will always bust

Some people feel that the 12 "brings out the 10s" and to just stand on all 12s or to stand on 12 against the dealer's 2. The likelihood is that a non-10-card is next is always greater than the likelihood that a 10-valued card is next. Remember that only 31 percent of a deck is composed of 10s.

This superstition is harmful to you if you follow it.

You should play your hands differently, depending upon whether the table is running hot or cold

There are definitely streaks in blackjack – good streaks, bad streaks, choppy streaks. You can lose 20 hands in a row, as I did, or you can win 20 hands in a row. However, when someone experiences a losing streak, the person right next to him can be experiencing a winning streak. The person next to her can be breaking even. Good, bad, and indifferent streaks are not predictable. Yes, there are times when the dealer turns every stiff hand into 20 and 21. There are times when the dealer busts like wild. Unfortunately, there is no way to predict when the busts will come or when the hits will come.

Speed Counters have slightly more insight into the probabilities in the remaining deck or decks because in high counts there will tend to be more 10-valued cards remaining than normal. In low counts, there are generally fewer 10-valued cards remaining on average. But that does not translate into perfect predictability, just a better probability.

In short, do not change the way you play your hands because of the recent streaks you or the dealer have been experiencing.

A player at third base should always take the dealer's bust card

I really wish that were an option. The player can volunteer to bust out in order to save the rest of us. But it isn't an option as the first superstition shows us.

I just lost 10 hands in succession so I'm due to win the next hand

You just lost those 10 hands and now you are in the position of the third baseman in the A-5 example above. Are you guaranteed a win on the next round? No, you aren't. You have a 50-50 chance of winning and a 50-50 chance of losing. Your streak has a 50-50 chance of ending and a 50-50 chance of continuing.

Changing the dealer will cause me to lose (or win)

Why? Will the new dealer change the order of the cards, the order of which no one on earth knows? The change of dealer has no effect on anything, unless the dealer is a card mechanic brought in to cheat you. That is unlikely to happen.

If the new dealer is nasty it might not be as pleasant playing with that dealer. But it has nothing to do with blackjack. That has to do with emotions and while emotions count, they don't count cards.

Bringing in new cards will cause me to lose (or win)

If you have been on a hot streak, you fear the new cards will cool you off. If you have been on a cold streak, what then? Will everything get hot? The new cards have nothing to do with anything, except they smell better than the old cards and are crisper and have less hand grease on them.

Only play at a blackjack table where the dealer is cold (or hot)

The dealer might have been as cold as Alaska in winter for the last hour or day or week. You sit down and there is no guarantee that the dealer will remain cold. Winter always ends, even in Alaska.

You must be a mathematical genius in order to win at blackjack

You have learned Speed Count and the OBS and you have taken all of our Golden Touch advice. You are now playing with an edge over the house – are you a genius? You might be but that has nothing to do with your ability to beat the casinos at blackjack.

You need a tremendous bankroll to win tremendous amounts of money

How do you make a small fortune in Las Vegas? You start with a large fortune.

Basic strategy players can be billionaires, so what? In the long run, they will lose. Now, for Golden Touch Blackjack players using proper bankroll-sizing techniques in accord with your Risk of Ruin calculations, then yes, to win a lot you must have a large bankroll. And, yes, to win large sums, you must bet large sums. But for the average basic strategy player and the average Ploppy, the question is: How do you make a small fortune in Vegas?

The objective of blackjack is to get to 21

No, no, no, the objective of blackjack is to beat the dealer. You can beat the dealer with a 12! Twenty-one is merely the highest level of card attainment before you go bust. It is not the aim of the game. The aim, once again, is to beat the dealer.

Betting progressions can overcome the house edge

No. Betting progressions can change the pattern of how you win and lose your money. In positive progressions, where you increase your bet when you win a hand, you will have many more losses since you are using part of your wins on your next bet. However, you will have some spectacular sessions when you win many hands in a row and get those bets to the sky.

In negative progressions, where you increase your bets when you lose a hand, you will have many more small winning sessions and a few spectacular losing sessions when you increase, lose, increase, lose, increase, lose and you ultimately get to table max – and lose again!

In the long run, you will lose the house edge on the totality of the money you wager. That's the fact behind this superstition.

Be wary of anybody, or book that claims you can win without card counting, or you can win by using just a betting progression system. There will always be those who claim you can win without card counting, but the math is the math... you gotta count to win at blackjack!

Always insure a good hand

If you have two 10s and the dealer has an ace as his up card, is it more or less likely that he will have a 10 in the hole to give him a blackjack? It is less likely since you have taken two 10-valued cards out of play. For Golden Touchers, there are hands that you will take insurance when the count gets to certain levels at the various games. Otherwise, the house has a nice fat edge on this bet – whether you have a good hand or a bad hand.

Take even money, since this guarantees that you will win

This is a "true" superstition that costs you money at the game. "Even money" is just another name for insurance. The dealer shows an ace, you have a blackjack and you take the one-to-one payoff rather than gamble that the dealer doesn't have a blackjack. This is a bad decision. The dealer only has an approximately 30 percent chance to have a 10 in the hole, since you have taken one 10 out of play. So 30 percent of the time you will win even money on your blackjack when the dealer also has a blackjack. The other 70 percent of the time you also win just even money, instead of 3 to 2.

Now if you didn't insure, you would break even on the 30 hands that the dealer had a blackjack. But on the 70 percent of the hands you would win 3 to 2. You make more money by not taking even money!

You have to have a photographic memory in order to count cards in the casino

Traditional card counting does not require a photographic memory – it requires you to remember a lot of elements as explained earlier in this book and none of these elements have to do with remembering the card pictorially. Speed Count in particular, since it doesn't require on-the-fly subtraction, requires even less mental skill to master.

Card counters have a big advantage in blackjack tournaments

Tournament blackjack is a whole different animal than counting cards in a normal game against the house. In tournaments you are playing against your fellow players. There will be times you must bet big to catch someone or protect your lead and it doesn't matter what the count is at these times. There may be times when you bet small, or take the low, when everyone else bets big – even if the count is high - in the hopes that the dealer beats the table. Card counting is not necessary or even all that useful to be a good tournament player.

It's impossible to win at blackjack. It is a game of luck

Actually, this isn't a superstition but a statement of fact for almost all blackjack players. While playing correct basic strategy will cut that house edge down to a minimum, the house will still have a small edge over you. The math of the game will dictate that the players lose in the long run. Those of you playing Golden Touch Blackjack will be the exceptions to this truth. You will have the edge over the house and the math will favor you in the long run. That blackjack can be beaten with card counting is a mathematical fact proven for over 40 years now.

- Chapter 10 -
Blackjack Questions

Question 1: Should Golden Touch Blackjack players tip the dealers?

Henry Tamburin: If you are a $10 Golden Touch Blackjack player your expectation is to win around $7.50 per hour (assuming good rules, decks and/or penetration). This profit can be easily negated by over tipping. However, if your dealer is friendly and makes your playing session enjoyable and you want to tip for good service here's a way to do it that will save you money. Place a dollar chip on top of your chips in the betting circle and tell the dealer, "This is for you." If the hand wins give the dealer the winning dollar chip and let the original dollar chip ride on the next hand. As long as you keep winning, so will the dealer. Tipping in this manner will also give you a slightly higher average bet for rating purposes. Quarter and black chip Golden Touch Blackjack players have higher win rates so they can afford to tip more ($5 tip bet is suggested).

In fact tipping at that betting level is good camouflage because the casino's stereotype of a card counter is someone who never tips. In casinos where dealers have some leeway in where they position the cut card after the shuffle (i.e., the penetration), a tip now and then might also influence them to position that cut card slightly deeper than normal. Timing a tip can also help. If the count is high and a relief dealer arrives at the table, making a tip bet for your dealer might influence her to deal out one more hand before relinquishing the cards to the relief dealer.

Dominator: Many card counters have this thing about not tipping as if tipping is bad. There are many careers where tips are the main salary ingredient – waiters, waitresses, barbers, maids, valet parkers – and also dealers. If the dealers were paid a living wage, the cost of the games would go up and you would not have any $10 tables left. A small tip for a good dealer should be factored into your playing scheme.

Frank Scoblete: I tip good dealers. It's their livelihood and reward for good service. However, $5 players have to be very careful about tipping since your edge is small. But if you are a $25 or $100 player, then by all means, give some modest tips each half hour.

Question 2: I have trouble keeping the count; help me!

Frank Scoblete: Some people do have trouble keeping the Speed Count in the noisy casinos – especially when they first begin playing as an advantage player. Don't fret. There's an easy way to keep the count, which I will explain to you shortly. But first, what usually makes someone easily forget the Speed Count is putting other numbers in their head that compete with the Speed Count number – like adding up the hands of the other players and the dealer. So my first piece of advice is avoid doing this – just keep track of the small cards and the Speed Count in your head and nothing else.

You can keep the count with your chips. Make sure you have several piles of chips in front of you – and make sure those piles are composed of chips of different colors. You'll want some one-dollar chips too – maybe 10 to 20 of them. Have some of the chips spilling over. You want to be a little bit of a pig here. One pile of the few in front of you is your counting pile. If you are playing a double-deck game, you can have a green chip with a red one on top. That is your initial count of 30. When the next round is finished you can add ones to that pile if the count went up or take off the red chip and add ones to give you the numbers 26, 27, 28, 29. You can even have a couple of reds under the green chip to make this pile look as messy as the other piles. Indeed, if you have four reds under the green chip and the count should dip under 25, you can take the green chip off. Remember when those cards are being dealt out, you can fiddle with your chips since you aren't interested in other people's draws.

What you don't want in front of you are several piles of neatly stacked chips with each denomination being its own pile and then you have that one messy one with different colors. That looks weird and might even look suspicious.

Sometimes if you have played too long, your mind can get fuzzy and you'll find yourself daydreaming and losing the count. That is the time to quit the session and take a walk or a nap.

Henry Tamburin: When you practice at home, you should have a noisy environment to simulate what happens in the casinos (e.g., practice with the TV or radio on). That can be helpful to you. The casino atmosphere does not make it easy to think. They don't want you to think. So mimic that in your practice sessions.

Dan Pronovost: Use our free training software that comes with this book to practice Speed Count (see page 115). The software will tell you when you're right or wrong, so you know when you're ready to hit the casinos.

Question 3: Is it wise to play with other Golden Touchers or card counters at the same table?

Dominator: I hate to ride the fence with this question, but the answer is yes and no. First let's talk about why this isn't a good idea. When two Golden Touch card counters are at the same table, chances are that both of you will be increasing your bets at the same time, and worse, the same amount. This can look very suspicious to the pit critters. The beauty of the Golden Touch method of card counting is not only the simplicity of the system, but also you will be making bets sooner than a normal High-Low card counter would. But two people increasing their bets at the same time just isn't a good idea.

If you are going to play with other Golden Touch players at the same table, you should not bet the same way. You must vary how you spread your bets so you don't look as if you are following the same script. We use a way of betting that allows us to move bets around in low counts so our players are never betting the same way. My minimum bet might be a hundred dollars but I will bet 80 or 110 or 75 or 95, while my friend will bet 100, 75, 95 or 110. You mix it up. Also in high counts, you never want to peak your bets at the same level. It is more dangerous to play with other Golden Touchers at the tables and you might want to only give yourselves a half hour at any one table doing this.

Frank and I will play together at the same table as a team. But before we start we have a pre-defined method of increasing our bets as I have shown. We also have a predefined way of acting at the tables that will throw off the pit critters. So if you want to play with another Golden Touch card counter, you must have a plan and stick to it as you play.

Frank Scoblete: You are better off never playing at tables with other card counters – it tends to bring attention to the table with everyone raising their bets at the same time. That's not *too* obvious! You might be doing just fine but the other counter brings the attention and an accident catches you too. It is best, when all is said and done, to play without other counters at the table. Of course, I have played with other Golden Touchers at the table using Dominator's advice above. But you must be very careful even with other Golden Touchers at the same table.

Henry Tamburin: I stay away from other counters when I play. Many counters, especially beginners, give out too many signals that they are keeping track of the cards and bring too much attention to our table

Question 4: I know in craps that Frank has many tricks to increase one's average bet without the monetary risk involved. Are there any comp tricks for blackjack?

Frank Scoblete: As a Golden Touch Blackjack player, you are playing with an edge over the casino. Let us say you are playing with a 0.4%-percent edge over the house. You win 40 cents for every $100 you bet. Now the casino rates you as losing two dollars for every $100 you bet because most casinos traditionally figure blackjack players to be facing a 2 percent house edge. The casino will return about 40 percent of your loss in the form of comps. So you get 80 cents in comps for every $100 you bet. Let us say you are a $10 Golden Touch player. The casino will rate you as playing about $20 per hand (remember they figure your increases in high counts as part of your betting) and you play about 100 hands an hour, that's $2,000 in action. You win $8 per hour from your edge. You also get $16 per hour in comps. As a $10 Golden Toucher you are now winning $24 from the casinos every hour. If you are a $50 player, just multiply these figures by five.

Here is some more information, slightly borrowed from *Golden Touch Dice Control Revolution!* by Dominator and me.

The casinos have staffs of expert psychologists, psychiatrists and public relations people hunkering in underground bunkers where they figure out ways to fuel the players' desire to be loved, appreciated and desired. These "psychos" are expert at making gamblers bet more, play more, lose more – and seemingly enjoy it more. And all the casino bosses, shareholders, and executives laugh at the foolish gamblers trying to overcome Lady Luck's capriciousness. And the money rolls in!

Okay, that paragraph was a little over the top. Most of the "psychos" are actually above ground. The rest of that paragraph is thematically true, if not also literally true.

The casinos beat gamblers with the house edge on their games, with their massive bankrolls, and with their ability to get the players to almost enjoy throwing their money away. One of the best tools in the casinos' psychological warfare with the players is the area of comps – those supposed freebies given to loyal players. Comps are the biggest weapon in getting people to gamble more than they want and sometimes more than they ought.

Comps are used to make casino gamblers want to be recognized, loved, appreciated, lionized, and revered. All those red-chip players look at the comps of the green-chip players and are envious. Green-chip players look at black-chip players and are envious. Black-chip players look at purple-chip players who are looking at orange-chip players who are looking at gold-chip players who are looking at brown-chip players who are thinking of the late Kerry Packer, who was treated as a god – and everyone wishes to be worshipped like that.

The big RFB comps (room, food, board) – that is, comps for everything: your room, food, drinks, shows, limos, shopping sprees, and exclusive parties – are the nectar of the gambling gods and even the lowliest player wishes to partake.

And how dopey is that? Completely and utterly.

Comps are meaningless if you are losing your money to the casino. So what if they are giving some of your money back to you in the form of comps – you are still a loser. But for some unfathomable reason, casino gamblers are in love with comps. They think, perhaps, that comps tell them something important about themselves, when in fact the casino would comp a bum who bet and lost enough to "merit" it. In fact, in my book *Best Blackjack* is the true story of the "million dollar bum" who received incredible comps while on a winning streak at Treasure Island. When he started losing…well, read the story. It's funny and educational.

Needless to say but necessary to say nevertheless, comps are a waste of time pursuing if they cost more to get than they return. If you are expected to lose $5,000 based on your level of betting, the fact that the casino might return $2,000 in the form of comps just means you are a $3,000 loser.

Let's go through how this works.

The formula for the monetary edge is simple: Comps + money win/loss = monetary edge. Most casinos will give back between 30 and 50 percent of your expected *theoretical loss* in the form of comps. Your theoretical loss is not your actual loss. On any given trip you can win and still be considered a loser – or you can lose much more than your theoretical loss as well.

The formula for comps:

Avg. Bet X Number of Decisions Per Hour X Number of Hours You Play X House Edge = Theoretical Loss

Casinos rate blackjack players as losing about 2 percent of their total action (house edge in above formula). Once they plug in the rest of the numbers in the formula they calculate your theoretical loss and then give you between 30-50 percent of that in comps.

Casinos love to use psychology against the players; it helps the bottom line. But players can also psych out the casinos in the comping game. We want the casinos to rate us as bigger bettors than we actually are and/or we want to get more comps than we actually have earned. Here are some helpful hints to achieve our goals:

1. Always tip on top of your bet, not in front of it. Henry already explained this technique, but it's worth repeating. Keep that bet riding for dealers; never take it off or give it to them, but let them know that bet is theirs if you keep winning. By doing this, the bet counts as a part of your bet, increasing your average bet. If you tip any other way, the bet does not count as a part of your bet. Also, you are only wagering a single bet that can win over and over again if you get on a hot streak. On other types of tips, the casino dealers take both the tip and the win down. To keep the dealers in action you have to make tip after tip after tip. You are spending more this way and receiving no benefit.

2. Always ask for a comp at least 10 minutes before you plan to leave a table. Let the rater think he has kept you at the

table longer than you planned to be there. That helps you look stupid.

3. The BIG Bet ploy: If you want to occasionally put up a "show bet" that is substantially bigger than your normal starting bet to get that in your rating, then do it while the dealer is shuffling. It will be up longer, seen more readily by the rater, and not be at risk. Sometimes if the rater goes to another table, you can even take the bet down – and have no risk and a nice rating.

4. If you are a "marginal RFB/RLFB" and you are staying at a property, do not put everything on your room and wait until the end to find out what they will comp. Instead – *comp as you go.* Many times you will be able to get café and buffet comps up front and then get the total theoretical loss at the end of your stay to put against your gourmet food as well.

5. If you have stopped playing and have asked for a comp; stay at the table. Let them ask you to move. The fact that you are taking up a space will motivate "the computer" to work faster on your comps.

6. If you are an RFB player and are interested in getting airfare for your play but have been turned down in the past, ask the casino to put you in a regular room and not a suite. Usually the suites are about five to 10 times more expensive. If you stay in a regular room, you might reduce what the casino figures they have spent on you and they just might give you your airfare.

7. The "Casino Psychology Departments" use comps as a way to *get you* to measure your "self-worth" based on how many comps you get and what a big shot you are for getting them. No comp is worth the loss of money or sleep. Play your game and the comps will come or they won't. Use our tricks too because they can't hurt!

Dominator: Frank gives great advice about comps but when all is said and done you are playing to beat the house.

The comps will come or they won't come. Your main aim is to be an advantage player.

Question 5: Don't the casino raters respect people who bet big?

Dominator: Some casino players really think that the size of their bets can get the casino personnel to think of them as big shots. Nothing could be farther from the truth. Is a person playing a game where he must lose, a smart person? I'd say, no, that's pretty stupid behavior if you ask me. Just betting bigger is even stupider behavior because bigger bets mean bigger losses. Are the casino personnel really impressed by dopes willing to lose big money – even though these dopes get great comps that cost them a fortune in losses? I'd say they are disdainful of such people. How can they be impressed by such stupidity?

Frank Scoblete: You play a game you can't beat and you want respect for that? Are you crazy?

Question 6: Can you explain the value of uneven betting?

Henry Tamburin: Uneven betting is great camouflage that costs nothing. There are two types. Instead of betting say three green chips on one hand when the count increases, put out a rainbow of different colored chips in your betting circle (like two greens, five reds, and a pink chip or some dollars). The later looks a lot less onerous than three green chips. Fumbling around as you stack your rainbow also gives the perception that you don't know what you are doing. Another type of uneven betting which also is good camouflage is to bet uneven amounts when you spread to two hands. So instead of betting exactly two green chips on one hand and two greens on another hand when the count increases, bet uneven amounts (like $40 on one hand and $60 on the other hand). You are still betting a total of $100 on the two hands but in a manner that is not as traditional. Many card counters are too neat and by being the opposite of neat, you will not look like a card counter.

Frank Scoblete: Uneven betting is great and also being sloppy with your chips is great. These are the techniques of the Ploppies and they are wonderful for making you look less than what you are. If you play two hands pretend that you are using some kind of progression betting and always have more on one hand and less on the other hand. This is a great way to bet.

Question 7: You have mentioned that it is a good to use the OBS cards at the table. Can you give me examples of why you think doing so is helpful?

Dominator: I just love to tell this story about what actually happened to me at the tables because I always have the Golden Touch OBS card on the layout in front of me when I play. Having the Golden Touch OBS card with you, always makes you look like a stupid player and as a card counter, you want to look as stupid as you can get! Then, if a pit critter looks at the OBS card and sees some of the plays that are different compared to normal basic strategy, you will get all sorts of comments like: "You don't know what you are doing."

Even better! Let me tell you that I have been called or thought of as a stupid player more than once and I love it!

Now I will relate the ultimate "stupid" story. I am playing at a very well known and popular Strip casino in Las Vegas. I am playing their shoe game when I get dealt a two card total of eight and the dealer is showing a six. So I take a look at my OBS card and when it is my turn I put out a double down bet.

The dealer says to me, "Sir, are you sure that your card says to do that?"

I take another look at my card, use my fingers and go down the column and say, "Yes, it sure does!"

The dealer says to me, "Sir, where did you get that card because I have never seen that play before?"

I just love when they ask me that because I say, "Susan, I got this card from my grandfather. My grandfather brought this book over from Italy that had this blackjack strategy in it, and he always used it. Out of respect for my grandfather, I use it also. My grandfather always seemed to win, or at least that is what he told all of us."

The dealer gives me a shrug of her shoulders, deals me an ace and I win my double down. Now the pit critter lady comes over, not for anything more than just to watch the game as the casino was dead and I think she was bored. On the next shoe, I get dealt an ace-three against the dealer's four. I proceed to look at my card and proceed to put out my double down bet. The Pit lady says to me, "Sir, are you sure that your card says to do that?

I don't have to answer because the dealer says, "Oh yes Linda, and his card does say to do that. He got that card from his Italian grandfather."

Linda the pit critter says, "His grandfather should learn how to play blackjack!"

Now I am asking myself, should I act mad that Linda said that my grandfather, who never played blackjack in his life, didn't know how to play? Or should I just think that my camouflage is just so good and be happy they think of me as a complete idiot?

I wait till the end of the shoe to make my decision about Linda and then I can't resist. I call her over to the table and say to her, "Linda, I want two apologies from you. First you insinuate that I don't know how to play blackjack, and what difference does that make to you? Everyone at this table can bet their money anyway they want to. But more important, you insulted my grandfather, a WWII veteran, even though he fought for Mussolini, and I want an apology!" At this point this little old man next to me, who didn't say one word as we were playing, says in a very strong Italian accent, "You betta apologize to his grandfather, I fought under Mussolini too!"

The table went quiet and the apology was given with me smiling and saying to myself, "Thank you Golden Touch!"

Question 8: What is inverse betting? Is it a good way to bet?

Dan Pronovost: The basic principle of card counting is that, depending on the composition of the remaining cards to be dealt, either the casino has the edge or you have the edge. Hence, you should bet proportionately more when you have the edge, and as little as possible when the casino has the edge.

One way card counters typically get the most possible amount of money out when they have a healthy edge is to play more than one blackjack hand/spot in these cases. But this can impact your potential edge, in that more cards will be dealt out since you are playing more than one hand now. In blackjack, the edge will tend to come down when it is high, and tend to go up when it is low (the edge is a *dependent probability*). So, by playing more hands when the count is high (or the same number of hands all the time), the concern is that you will be "eating the good cards."

One way to avoid this is *inverse hand spreading*. To understand this, consider a typical range of bets, as the player's edge increases: 1, 2, 4 (bet units), all played on one hand (we call this a 1 to 4 bet ramp). With inverse hand spreading, our goal is to play many hands at a low count and fewer hands at high counts, while still leveraging the same bet spread. When the count is high, we will then be playing fewer hands but still betting the same amount of money. When the count is low, we will play more hands, but with the same minimum bet in effect. Another way to understand this is to remember that when the count is very high, it is more likely to come back down, and vice versa. So when it's high, let's play fewer hands to get more rounds and bets out at the high counts. We want to use the same bet ramp, so we end up with this potential way of betting and playing:

Low edge: three hands of one bet unit

Good edge: two hands three units

High edge: one hand of 12 units

This is a 3 to 12 bet spread, which is the same as our original 1 to 4 bet ramp. But, we will "eat" more cards when the count is bad (by playing three hands), and less when the count is high (by playing only one hand). I studied inverse hand spreading in detail in an article published online at *Blackjack Insider*:

http://www.bjinsider.com/newsletter_53_inv.shtml

In it, I show clearly that a card counter can get a nice increase in hourly win rate by using inverse hand spreading. But there are pragmatic issues, such as the fact that you must be comfortable playing with an effective minimum bet size at least three times the table minimum, and hope that the monstrous bets on one hand do not flag the attention of the pit bosses!

Using the above method, you can easily generate a suitable inverse bet spread for Speed Count. It works equally with all traditional card-counting systems that generate an edge based on the count.

Question 9: Are there any other betting methods that can camouflage what you are doing at the tables, which is betting more when you have the edge and less when the casino has the edge?

Frank Scoblete: Here is a betting strategy that is excellent. It's called "go up and go down." After the first shuffle, you start with your one unit and go to four units in a high count. If you get to four units that's great. However, after the next shuffle, you start at four units and if the count becomes favorable, you stay at four units. If the count goes down, you drop your bet with the count. In this way, you are not always going one to four but you are also going four to one.

You mix up how you play the rounds so that your betting style is never easily discerned. Mixing up your betting like this is unusual and very few card counters will do this.

Question 10: Are gambling coupons valuable? Can you go through some of the typical ones?

Henry Tamburin: Yes, gambling coupons are valuable because you will always have the edge over the house when you use them. The most common are the matchplay, bonus blackjack, and free ace coupons. A matchplay coupon works like this. Suppose you have a $10 matchplay coupon. Place the coupon in the betting circle and place $10 of your chips on top. If you win the hand the casino will pay you $10 for your $10 wager and another $10 for the matchplay coupon. Essentially the casino doubled your payout if the hand wins (i.e., you bet $10 and won $20). Most matchplay coupons can only be used for one hand and win or lose the casino will keep the coupon. The expected value of a $10 matchplay coupon is about $4.75 (probability of winning times face value of matchplay or 47.5 percent x $10).

The bonus blackjack coupon pays a bonus on your first blackjack. Instead of the usual 3-2 payoff you will get paid 3-1 or 2-1. You will get a blackjack on average about once in every 21 hands. The expected value of a 3-1 coupon is the amount wagered x (1.5 –21 x house edge). So if you wagered $25 with a 3-1 blackjack bonus coupon in a typical Las Vegas 2-deck blackjack game where the house edge over the basic strategy player is 0.4 percent, the value of the coupon is $35.40 ($25 x (1.5 – 21 x 0.004)). Another valuable blackjack coupon is the "Free Ace," which substitutes as an ace for your first card. To use it, just place the coupon on the layout with a bet and the dealer will skip over you the first time he deals around because your coupon represents an ace. If your next card is a ten or picture card, you automatically have a blackjack. These coupons usually specify the maximum amount you can wager along with the coupon (usually $5, $10 or $25). You have a big 55 percent edge using this coupon (assuming the free ace can be kept and replayed which is usually the case – if it can't your edge is 50.5 percent, which is also great). A good source of gambling coupons has been the *Pocketbook of Values* that subscribers to Anthony Curtis' *Las Vegas Advisor* automatically receive.

Dominator: When you get coupons from certain magazines, it does peg you as a more intelligent player than most of the Ploppies in the casino. You should just do coupon runs without playing too long in the casino where you are using the coupon – if you do return to that casino, return during a different shift.

Frank Scoblete: In the past, you could play opposite propositions with coupons – for example, you could bet a coupon on the Pass Line and your wife could bet her coupon on the Don't Pass line. Over the years casinos have become annoyed at this type of almost guaranteed win. So avoid being cute. Play the coupon properly. You really don't want to bring any attention to yourself.

Question 11: What does the eye-in-the-sky look for to figure out if someone is counting?

Henry Tamburin: All casinos have their own procedures but in general the casino surveillance personnel in the EITS (abbreviation for eye-in-the-sky) will first check if the player knows anything about basic strategy. If he doesn't, this might be enough for the EITS to conclude the player is not a counter. The second characteristic the EITS looks for is how the player is moving his money. Does he always bet the same amount at the start of the shoe and then increase his bets as play progresses? Does he spread to two hands with fairly large bets then drop to a smaller bet on one hand?

If they are still suspicious the EITS will check if the player deviates from basic strategy. Most trained EITS personnel know the hands that traditional counters will often deviate from basic strategy based on the count. One of the key hands they watch is a hard 16 against a dealer 10. Traditional counters will hit 16 when they bet small and stand on 16 when they bet large. Some casinos also use sophisticated software, which allows them to determine if the player is a counter based on inputting how he plays, and bets, or they will compare the player's facial characteristics to a casino database of known card counters. Our OBS makes you look like less than a good card counter since we do not change our plays based on the count. Our OBS improves our edge and makes us look somewhat stupid and as Frank says, "Stupid is good."

Question 12: When should I stop playing?

Dominator: Our advice is to limit your playing time per session to about 45 minutes to one hour simply because the longer you play the more time you give the casino to observe and analyze your playing characteristics. Other stopping points you might want to consider are after you spread to two (or more) hands with max bets at the end of the shoe or after you've gone through three to five cycles of your bet ramp. Playing a session for a short period of time is usually never a problem but playing too long at the table can be.

Henry Tamburin: You might exit after a really good run that has brought some attention your way. Say something like, "For once, I'm taking this win home with me!" and leave the casino.

Frank Scoblete: No matter what – win or lose or break even – stop when you feel tired. If you start forgetting the count, it's time for a break.

Question 13: What should you do if you have horrendous losing sessions?

Henry Tamburin: If you've lost 10 percent or more of your bankroll you should reevaluate your Risk of Ruin to determine if you need to lower your betting level because if you maintain the same betting level with a smaller bankroll your Risk of Ruin might be too high. The Speed Count software is a good tool to help you determine this. What you should not do is get gun shy and bet less than your top bet when the Speed Count calls for it. Many beginning counters fall into this trap. You must load your gun with bullets (chips) and fire away when the edge shifts in your favor each and every time you play otherwise you will never beat the game. You must also recognize the fact that you can lose in the short run when you have the edge. But overall your bankroll will grow over time even though in the short run it will fluctuate.

Frank Scoblete: Losing is part of the game. What I do when I lose is calmly go back to my room, curl up in the fetal position and suck my thumb.

Dominator: I curse, yell and scream, smoke a cigarette and then I feel fine and I am ready to play again.

Dan Pronovost: I eat.

Question 14: What should you do if you are playing a juicy two-deck game heads up, the count has skyrocketed, and a player walks up to the table ready to buy in?

Henry Tamburin: When you are an advantage player this is the worst possible time to have a new player join your game because you will get fewer hands dealt in a favorable situation prior to the shuffle. One thing you can do to discourage the new player from entering is to say something to the effect, "I hope you have a lot of money, 'cause Joe [the dealer] has been killing me." Most ploppies will heed your advice and move on. Another way to handle this situation is to simply ask the new player politely if he/she wouldn't mind waiting till after the shuffle before playing so you "don't change the flow of the cards." Getting as many hands dealt when the Speed Count is high prior to the shuffle is important to maintain a healthy edge over the house.

Frank Scoblete: If you turn to the new player and show them you have drool coming from your mouth down your chin dripping onto your shirt and then you talk incoherently, "Blah, dung, carps, nutta," that will often send them running to a different table.

Dominator: I yell, curse, scream and smoke a cigarette. That usually gets them to go to another table.

Dan Pronovost: I belch loud from all the food I ate. That usually turns them away.

Question 15: What should I do if the casino uses a six-deck shoe and cuts off half the decks?

Dominator: Don't play. Your edge will be miniscule at best so why bother? Head for the door and a new casino or, if you are on a boat, go up on deck and enjoy the view, even if it isn't so hot. Games with 50 percent penetration are a lot of work for very little return.

Dan Pronovost: I leave the casino and go have something to eat.

Question 16: Can several players use the Golden Touch Blackjack system as a team?

Dominator: I enjoy team play with certain individuals but you must be able to trust them to be honest. Most teams break up because several players get hot and win a lot of money and some players get cold and lose money and the hot players don't like sharing their wins. You can read about team play in a lot of blackjack books but it is a dangerous activity if the people are not trustworthy or if they are the suspicious types.

One way to play is to have what we call the "Opposite Gorilla." Most card counting teams bring in a Big Player (or Gorilla) to the table when the count is high. The Big Player bets big until the high count is over and then leaves. Casinos are aware of this tactic and watch for it.

What the Golden Touch team does is bring in a famous person who sits down at the table and gives his or her card in, and the casino floor person is aware of who this person is. Sometimes other players come over and ask for this person's autograph. However, our famous players, while they will vary their bets to keep the pit interested, are really only playing basic strategy – at other tables in the high roller room or at high-end tables will be our team players. So much attention goes to our Opposite Gorilla that the other counters are free and clear to play pretty aggressively since all attention is on the famous person. Even when our famous players are sometimes asked not to play, which rarely happens except in really paranoid casinos, that usually doesn't hurt the team because once the Opposite Gorilla leaves, the pit relaxes thinking they have done a great job of protecting their games and in fact the counters are hammering away at them for another hour or so. It's a great technique. Of course, you have to know famous people to have this work!

Frank Scoblete: Team play is fraught with problems, most of them regarding trust. In the beginning of your Golden Touch Blackjack career, I think you should get down playing alone before you even think of playing in a team or forming a team.

Question 17: Why don't you have index changes in the OBS like the other card counting systems do?

Dominator: Go into the corner, put this cap on, and listen up! The whole idea of Golden Touch Blackjack is for us to look UNLIKE the other advantage players. Everything we are doing here is to give you freedom to play under the radar – as best as we can manage it. The OBS allows us to maximize our edge while still allowing us to play the same way hand after hand (regardless of the Speed Count) just like regular players. It makes us look worse than the average basic strategy player too. Now, I will let you out of the corner if you listen to us carefully and follow our advice.

Frank Scoblete: The OBS is a brilliant way to play your hands. It increases your edge with Speed Count and makes you look dull.

Dan Pronovost: First, recognize that OBS is a partial substitute for index plays... they are designed to increase your edge yet are not as 'penalizing' as you'd think when compared to memorizing a whack of index plays. But most importantly, index plays are deceptively hard to learn and play correctly. Was that index -1 or +1? Was it on the hard 15, or 16? I generally tell people it will take them 40 to 80 hours to master a traditional count system like High-Low, but double that time if you include 30 or more indices. OBS gets you a large part of that increased edge, without the risk of errors AND give you some great camouflage! Lastly, the most useful index plays are also the ones that will give you away as a card counter to the casino, such as hard 16 versus dealer 10.

Question 18: Why don't you count the high cards instead of the low cards in Speed Count?

Dan Pronovost: Well, the simple answer is because I tried it in simulations, and it didn't work. In fact, I tried dozens of different simplified counts I invented, and only Speed Count as published worked as well with the ease of use. But, there is of course a more mathematical explanation.

Speed Count is an unbalanced count system, unlike High-Low but similar in mathematical properties to other unbalanced count systems like Knock-Out. This means that the counting metric does not directly reflect your edge in the game, and the count tends to 'drift' upwards. The latter property is essential in successful unbalanced count systems, and ideally the final average resting count (given an average penetration) should be close to the bet pivot. The bet pivot should be the count at which you have an edge, and good unbalanced counts should show a nice linear relationship to count and edge, as we show with Speed Count on page 32.

When you count the high cards, the edge does not drift in the right direction, nor do you get the nice correlation of edge to count. Even if you invert the count meaning, and treat low counts as higher edge (as would be expected if counting the tens and aces), things do not work out well. The main reason is that when there are many tens and aces, the average number of counted cards per hand is no longer as high as 2.7, and the 'trick' we depend on to make Speed Count work begins to fail. Ultimately, the correlation between the low cards and average number of cards per hand is stronger when counting 2 to 6, instead of 10s and aces, since high valued hands (from 17 to 21, for example) will tend to have very few cards (and the reverse is less true with low cards).

Question 19: Does the number of players have any effect on the power of Speed Count?

Dan Pronovost: Due to the unique counting concept of Speed Count, there is good reason to wonder if the number of players can have an impact on the performance of Speed Count. This is not as relevant with most other count systems, especially balanced methods such as High-Low. In the data analysis chapter on page 133, we show Speed Count simulations for both one and six player games across 40 different games. Generally, the differences in performance are marginal, and what we would expect in general. For example, the win rates (average earnings per round in bet units) for the 2 deck DAS/S17 games are 0.011103 and 0.009420 for one and six players respectively (a performance decrease of 15 percent). The respective edges and standard deviations (a measure of risk) are also fairly close. For the six deck DAS/S17 game, the win rates are 0.011992 and 0.007887 for one and six players respectively (a drop in performance of 34 percent). Note also that it is standard to see some drop in performance when you add more players with any count system, for several reasons. For example, in two deck games the extra players may mean fewer rounds dealt at deeper penetrations where you have the greatest edge potential.

Question 20: What percent of the time can I expect to increase my bets using Speed Count?

Dan Pronovost: The frequency histogram on page 33 shows the proportion of occurrences of rounds at different counts for a standard two-deck game. But let's look at the exact frequencies for yet another example, with four players. For a two deck DAS/S17 game with four players, rounds will start at a Speed Count of 31 or greater about 35 percent of the time. For the same respective six player game, the rate is about 27 percent. What is interesting to observe is that you have to be more patient when there are more decks, and bet more when you do have an edge to get a good earning rate. Don't be surprised in a six or eight deck game if the count never gets above 30. This is the nature of blackjack, and why good double-deck games (and the rare beatable single-deck game) are highly sought after by card counters. Of course, casinos know this and will tend to watch these games more closely than six and eight-deck games.

- Chapter 11 -
Final Word

The Golden Touch Blackjack system was designed so that average blackjack players can, with little effort, gain the edge over the casino. If you use the OBS, bet based on the Speed Count, and follow our advice on bankroll, Risk of Ruin, camouflage, and playing demeanor, you will become an advantage blackjack player and win more money than you will lose over time.

On page 115 you will find a tutorial on the Speed Count software that came with this book. By using this terrific software, you will be able to practice the OBS playing strategy and Speed Count betting in the comfort of your home. It's a terrific tool to hone your skills before playing for real money in a casino.

The Appendices in this book contain:

- A summary of the computer simulation data for Speed Count that proves it gives you the edge over the casino in virtually all games.
- A summary of the Golden Touch Blackjack one and two day hands-on courses where you will play and learn under the tutelage of our professional instructors.
- Information on our Golden Touch Blackjack DVD with Dr. Henry Tamburin, Dominator and Frank Scoblete showing you step-by-step how to get the edge at blackjack.
- Information on our OBS strategy cards that allow you to have the correct playing strategy at your fingertips when you play (while appearing to be a novice player).
- A tutorial on how to play blackjack for players with no or very little playing experience.

- Information on our Golden Touch Craps course that will teach you dice control and allow you to have the edge in a second game.
- Information on the *Blackjack Insider Newsletter*, a monthly e-publication of new articles on gambling by top industry authors.

I've come to the end of what I have to say about a truly remarkable, revolutionary system that allows average players to easily beat the casino at blackjack. Enjoy your new skills and the fantastic, confident feeling that you will have knowing that every time you walk into a casino, you now have the skills to beat them at their own game.

Winning is the most fun.

- Appendix 1 -
Speed Count Training Software

So, that CD in the back of this book... does it really contain free Speed Count training software?!

Yes. Not shareware, not nagware, not adware... fully functional software with Speed Count training drills.

The software is a custom version of *Blackjack Counter* for Windows by DeepNet Technologies (**www.HandheldBlackjack.com)**, tailored just for Speed Count.

When you've exhausted the features in the limited software version provided with this book, you can choose to purchase additional blackjack training programs and packages from DeepNet. The full version of *Blackjack Counter* allows you to customize count systems, try other count systems (including High-Low and many others), and even use the handheld PDA versions for Palm OS© or Microsoft Pocket PC© devices. *Blackjack Expert* is also available, where you actually play blackjack and can have some or all of your decisions tested for accuracy. And for players looking for the most advanced tools, you can also purchase *Blackjack Audit,* the simulator used to develop Speed Count, which also includes Risk of Ruin calculators and features. Many packages are available at different prices for different platforms, which bundle the components listed above. Visit the web site for details: **www.HandheldBlackjack.com**.

Software Requirements

The software will work on any Microsoft Windows computer with Windows 98 or higher. *Blackjack Counter* and *Expert*, our two main training products, are available for Palm OS and Pocket PC (**www.HandheldBlackjack.com)**, but are not included in the Speed Count free version with this book. About 10 megabytes of hard disk storage is required to install the software.

Installing the Software

Just insert the CD into your Windows computer CD-ROM drive, and the installation program will start automatically. If it does not, use 'My computer' to explore the CD drive, and run the 'setup.exe' program.

Follow the prompts to install *Blackjack Counter* to your computer. A program group is created, and a shortcut to start *Blackjack Counter* is put on your desktop.

Questions?

The best place to get help is right in the software, from the help menu. Also, a special help screen is displayed to the right of the main program that lists the common help topics. And lastly, you can always press the 'F1' key anywhere, anytime, to get specific help on the feature or dialog.

If you're still stuck, check out our web site for more information and our FAQ (frequently asked questions): **www.HandheldBlackjack.com**.

Speed Count Software for Dumb-Dumbs

This section is intended as a step-by-step tutorial to help you get the most out of the *Blackjack Counter* training software right away. After you've installed the software, run *Blackjack Counter* and follow along with this tutorial.

Starting Blackjack Counter for the first time

When you first start *Blackjack Counter*, you'll see a screen like the one that follows. Yours will show a different set of cards since the drills are random, but otherwise it will be the same.

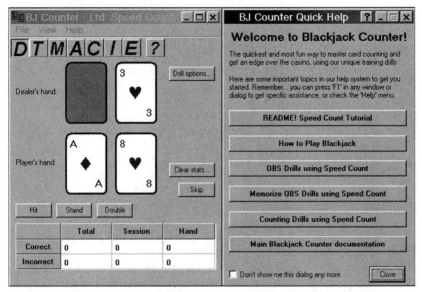

On the left is the main program window. The right window displays our 'Quick Help' guide, which contains some helpful information including this tutorial. Once you are familiar with *Blackjack Counter*, you can click the 'Don't show me this dialog any more' checkbox near the bottom of the Quick Help window, and close it. If you want to see the Quick Help dialog again, you can do so from the Help menu in the main program.

Quick Help Dialog

See those buttons in the Quick Help window? Guess what they are for.... That's right! They are aides for you to figure out how to use the program, which are quick.

The first one is a link to this stunning tutorial. No, it's not going to magically open your *Golden Touch Blackjack Revolution!* book to this page, but instead it will bring up an 'online help' dialog version of this same text (in fact, you'll find these same exact words magically transformed onto your screen).

So, you've read the online help, but want to go back to the program? Just click (with your mouse) on the 'X' in the upper right of the online help window... the help window is closed and *Blackjack Counter* is brought to the front again. In fact, it was always there quietly waiting to help you become a better Speed Counter. You could choose to *minimize* the online help window instead by clicking on the flat icon to the left of the 'X' icon. This hides the online help window and puts an icon on your *taskbar* you can click on to bring it back.

Am I already over your head? Not sure whether the mouse is for entertaining your cat or using your computer? Then you probably need some more basic assistance on using Windows that is beyond the scope of this book (see the *Golden Touch Windows Revolution*, coming to theatres near you soon). But seriously… if you are new to using your computer and things like icons, taskbars, and menus sound like things in a restaurant more than computer terms, then you can purchase one of many basic Windows help books at your local computer or book store.

Are you new to blackjack… thought 21 referred to the legal drinking age in your state? Click the 'How to Play Blackjack' button. This is the same wonderful content in the corresponding chapter later in this book (see page 147).

The other buttons are just shortcuts into the online topics below.

Help! I've fallen (in the software), and can't get up!

Still confused in the software? Not sure what some feature or dialog is all about? Then just press 'F1' on your keyboard, and some *context sensitive* online help will appear before your eyes. There are reams of pages of documentation on every feature in the program, all available from the Help menu as well.

Users should note though that the core of the online help is for the general version of *Blackjack Counter*, not this limited Speed Count version. The general version supports all card counting systems, and has lots of extra features. So, don't be surprised when you press F1 if you learn a lot more!

Consider it a free taste of the exciting features available if you purchase the full version of *Blackjack Counter.*

Blackjack Counter Modes

Blackjack Counter has several different *modes* to help you practice. These modes correspond to the big lettered buttons you see below the menu:

- **D: Drill Mode.** Basic strategy drills.

- **T: Table Mode.** Shows the basic strategy table you are using right now, and statistics.

- **M: Memorize Mode.** Fill-in-the-blanks basic strategy training.

- **A: Action Mode.** Where you select the basic strategy table to use.

- **C: Count Mode.** Practice the Speed Count counting method here.

- **I: Index Mode.** Only available in the full version of *Blackjack Counter.*

- **E: Expert Mode.** Only available in the full version of *Blackjack Expert.* Play real blackjack, and the computer slaps your wrist when you make mistakes.

To switch modes, just click on the big corresponding lettered icon.

Ok… we tried to convince Dan to give you readers all of his great software away for free. Well, the lead balloon only sank half way to the ground, and Dan agreed to give you a bunch of amazing training features for free, but held a bunch back for those willing to shell out a few more bucks. For example, clicking on the **I** or **E** icons will bring up a dialog like this:

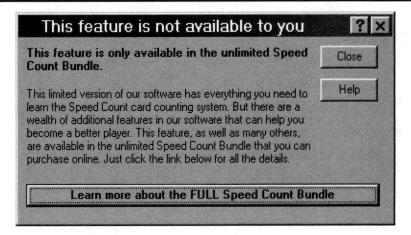

So stop being a cheapskate and click the button to browse Dan's full software catalogue, ok? You can buy the unlimited version of *Blackjack Counter* for just $25, or step up to one of his many money-saving bundles for a bit more. Click the button, or visit their web site:

http://www.handheldblackjack.com/bjscbundle.shtml

Still have doubts? Incredibly, you can try out any of the DeepNet training products for free (not just for blackjack, but craps and poker too). It's all up there for free trial download. Buy it only if you like it. Dan tells us that this is called *shareware*, which is a geek term meaning "you can try out the software for free, and it will annoy you the more you use it, until you buy it, after which you'll receive a *registration code* by e-mail to put in the software to remove these *nags*."

Drill Mode

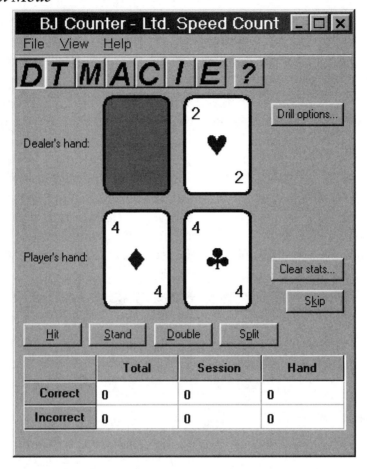

In Drill Mode, random blackjack hands are displayed, and you must click on the right action (i.e., hit, stand, double or split). This is basic strategy training at its best, and the fastest way to master those 300 odd OBS plays in the OBS chapter. To help in this learning process, *Blackjack Counter* will tend to ask you the hands that you answer incorrectly more often (*biased* drills).

The table below the action buttons shows you how well you've done so far. The *Total* column shows you your accuracy on all drills for all the times you've run *Blackjack Counter*. The *Session* column shows you your accuracy for only this execution of *Blackjack Counter*. The *Hand* column shows you your lifetime accuracy on only this one hand combination.

By default, the software is pre-configured with the OBS for multi-deck (two or more decks), DAS, and S17. You can change this though to any of the OBS tables, in Action Mode.

To specify an action, just click on the corresponding button. *Split* will only show up if you have a pair. If you don't want to use your mouse, just use the underlined letters for each corresponding button (h=hit, s=stand, d=double, p=split). Suppose you click on 'Hit' with the 4-4 vs. 2 hand displayed on page 121. This is wrong of course, and the software will reach out and scold you, as well as show you the correct OBS when you are dealt a pair of 2's against all dealer upcards (see below). Notice the correct OBS strategy for 2-2 against the dealer's 4 upcard is highlighted (P for split).

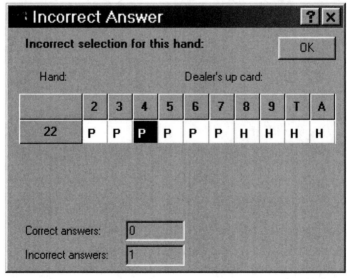

Click the 'OK' button, and you are returned to Drill Mode and a new random hand is displayed. Don't be surprised if the same hand is displayed again, since it will tend to quiz you more often on the hands you got wrong.

Don't want to answer a displayed hand? Click 'Skip'. Too embarrassed with your lousy results and want to start fresh? Click on 'Clear stats'. Then click on 'OK', or you can change the 'Tests' option to also change which hands you are tested on. You can also individually select the testing hands in Table Mode (see page 124), which is handy for picking only the toughest cases once you have mastered the obvious ones.

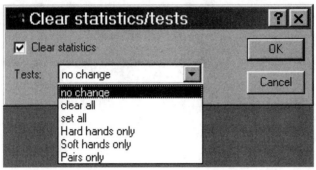

Table Mode

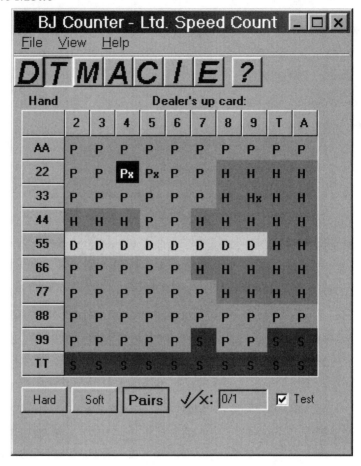

Table Mode shows you the whole OBS. Click on the 'Hard', 'Soft' or 'Pairs' button to show these subsets of the corresponding strategy.

See those 'x's beside the table entries? That means you've answered that question wrong before. Click on that cell entry, and the right/wrong field in the lower right of the window is updated to show you your lifetime statistics.

An advanced feature you may find useful is to customize which hands you are tested on in Drill Mode. Just click on the cell, and then set the 'Test' checkbox in the lower right acccordingly (check it if you want to be tested on that play combination, or clear it otherwise). You can also choose the row label to the left, and clear or set a whole row at a time. Alternatively, choose 'Preferences' from the File menu, then 'Stats/tests', and you can preselect a category of hands for testing (hard, soft, etc.).

Memorize Mode

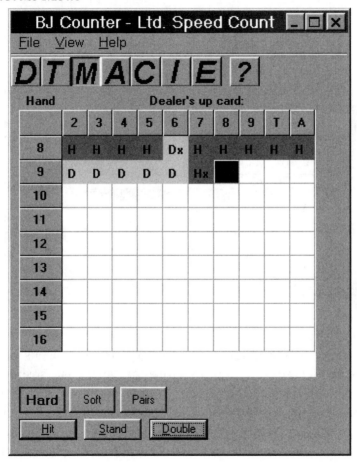

Memorize Mode is a great way to start off learning OBS. Click on 'Hard', 'Soft' or 'Pairs' to select the table to practice. Now, just enter the correct action for the hilighted cell. If you get it wrong, it will prompt you and display the entry with an 'x' beside it. You can click on any particular cell, or just follow along in order.

Action Mode

Action Mode is where you select the OBS table to use and train with. As you now know, the correct basic strategy depends on the rules of the game. We have provided eight OBS tables for Speed Count, covering the combinations of single-deck versus multi-deck (two or more decks), DAS/noDAS, and S17/H17. Click on the 'Table' button to select the different available tables.

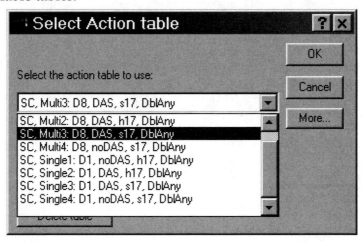

The eight OBS tables are available in the drop down list. Note that the 'Multi' tables are for two or more decks (it says D8 meaning eight-decks, but we use the same basic strategy for two to eight-decks with Speed Count). 'DblAny' means there are no doubling restrictions (restrictions on doubling, such as only on 10 or 11, are very bad for the player, and should be avoided). The remaining text shows the corresponding blackjack rules. So if you want to practice the OBS for a six deck game with s17 and das you would select: SC, Multi3: D8, s17, DblAny. Likewise, for a single-deck game with h17 and noDas you would select: SC, Single1: D1; noDas, h17, DblAny.

In the full version of *Blackjack Counter*, you can create your own basic strategy tables, load or purchase new ones, or

edit your own. None of these features are available in the Free
Speed Count version.

Count Mode

Once you've memorized your OBS in Drill and
Memorize Mode, you can start to practice the mechanics of
Speed Count in Count Mode. The real fun starts in Count
Mode, and it will tell you when you're really ready to hit the
casinos. The basic gist of Count Mode is that completed rounds
of blackjack are dealt out with a dealer hand and a few player
hands, and you have to track the Speed Count, and correctly
indicate it.

First, you can select the kind of counting drill you want to practice. Click on the 'Options' button:

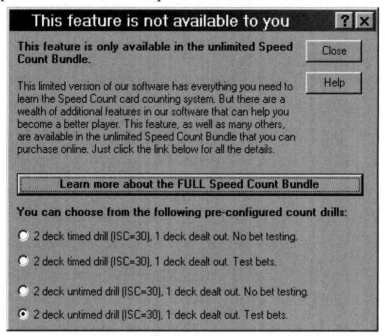

In the full version of *Blackjack Counter*, you can configure your counting drills in an amazing variety of ways. Press F1 to see online help that shows you all the options available in the full version. For the free Speed Count version, you can only select from one of four drill types: timed and un-timed, and with or without bet testing. In all four cases, we are testing with a two deck game, Conservative Speed Count, and dealing out 50 percent of the cards (this is a one-deck count down drill). This means you always start the Speed Count at 30 (the ISC for two deck games).

In the un-timed drills, each round is displayed and you enter the new Speed Count (and appropriate bet for the next round). In timed drills, each round is displayed for a few seconds, until 50 percent of the cards are dealt. Then, you enter the final Speed Count (and appropriate bet for the next round).

Click 'Close' to return to Count Mode, and then 'Start'. A summary dialog is displayed telling you what you are going to be tested on (check the box along the bottom to not have this help dialog displayed anymore). A game tableau like the one at the start of this section is displayed.

The round is shown played out. The dealer hand is to the left, with a few player hands to the right. You'll find that the software will change the number of player hands, just to keep you on your toes... so look carefully to determine how to adjust the Speed Count for the next round!

In the example shown on page 127, assuming this is the first round, we start with an ISC of 30, add three for the 2, 4 and 6, and subtract 3 for the three hands (including the dealer). This leaves us with a final Speed Count of 30. Click on '3' in the first row below the cards, and then zero on the second row. Or, type in 30.

If the Speed Count you entered is incorrect, then an error dialog is displayed, and you must re-enter it. If you're stumped, click on the 'Stats' button, and all the current count system information is displayed. It's the 'Run Count' field that displays the actual Speed Count (since *Blackjack Counter* is designed to work with any count system, there are a lot of fields in this form that do not apply to Speed Count). If you're baffled why the count is what it is you can click the 'Repeat same test' button (trust the software... it's far more likely you're wrong, not it!). This will reset the count mode and clicking 'Start' will repeat the same exact shoe of cards. If you find a bug in the software, tell Dan and he'll send you one of his famous hero sandwiches via dogsled courier.

If you have selected to be tested on bets, then a betting dialog is displayed after you enter the correct count:

Enter bet size ? ✕

Select the unit bet size for the current count:

1	2	3	4	5	6	7	8	9	10
11	12	13	14	15	16	17	18	19	20

Skip bet entry

Enter the correct bet size, in bet units. The table on page 24 shows you the correct betting strategy for Speed Count Conservative and two decks. You bet one unit at Speed Count 30 and less, two units at 31, and four units at 32 and higher. For our example, a Speed Count of 30 means we should bet 1 unit for the next round, so click on the '1' button. An error dialog is displayed if you get the answer incorrect. If you don't want to test yourself on this bet, click on the 'skip bet entry' button.

At the end of the drill, a statistics dialog is displayed that tells you how many errors you made. When you complete three timed count mode drills in a row without errors, you are doing quite well. Until then, practice more. Either way, you should consider purchasing the full version of *Blackjack Counter* so that you can tweak the counting drills to help you master every nuance of Speed Count (for example, you can shorten the display time with timed drills).

Note that with timed drills, you **only** enter the count and bet for the final displayed round. Do not click the count buttons until the rounds are finished being displayed.

Index Mode and Blackjack Expert

Speed Count does not use play indices, so Index Mode is not included in this free software. Play indices are hard to learn, but when used properly without errors in count systems such as High-Low, they can increase your edge over the casino.

Blackjack Expert is a separate training program from DeepNet Technologies. In it, you actually play real blackjack against the computer. While you play, it checks all your answers, and warns you when you make mistakes. *Blackjack Expert* works in tandem with *Blackjack Counter*, reading and using the count systems and settings from it. You can choose exactly what you want to be tested on, and select from a huge number of professional casino game options and formats. *Blackjack Expert*, which includes support for Speed Count, is available online:

http://www.handheldblackjack.com/bjscbundle.shtml.

- Appendix II -
Speed Count Simulation Data

A Few Words From Dan Pronovost

Munch, munch, chew, gulp.

Oh oh, readers reading! Better put down my hero sandwich and write something interesting. Simu, fetch me my computer from the igloo Up North, you digital canine, so I may bring forth data for the masses to drown in!

Ok, that's about as much wit the geek shall force upon you. Frank asked me to write up this technical section to fend off the few who demand, "More data! More proof! More sims!"

Inventing a new simplified blackjack card counting system is easy. Most well known books include a passing section with some trimmed down method usually titled something like, "A Really Useless Card Counting System for Dummies, Since Losers Always Ask Me For One." The results usually equal the effort and authors' interest: poor. Professional blackjack card counters scoff at simplified strategies, since they have mastered something that clearly performs better. Anything less powerful is a waste of time, stupid, or a fraud. With such an attitude, it's no wonder the 'easy' card counting systems to date have been virtually useless.

Professional players disdain average gamblers. I instead look at average gamblers, who play at a loss, as candidates in need of education. And in need of having something simple and fun instead of taxing... comics instead of Shakespeare, Mark Twain instead of Plato.

As such, I spent a lot of time inventing and refining Speed Count to be as powerful as possible, yet very easy to use. The hard part is not coming up with the card counting method, but proving it works and is easy to use in a pragmatic way.

So, I modified my own company's blackjack simulator product, *Blackjack Audit* (cheap plug alert...

www.HandheldBlackjack.com) to support the counting concept of Speed Count (no simulators at the time supported this, since the metric of counting cards per dealt hand was unheard of). From there, I noodled with all kinds of variations of the method, counting low cards, high cards, tweaks for blackjacks, twists for dealer hands, etc. The result is what you see in this book, which I have gladly (for you and me) left to Frank to present to you, fine reader.

I ran billions, and billions of simulations (about a trillion all in all, actually), testing all kinds of games and situations. Due to the unusual counting metric of Speed Count, I wanted absolute proof that the method would work well in different situations. What happens with more players, fewer players, more depth, different rules, more decks, fewer decks, etc.? And incredibly, Speed Count holds it own and works surprisingly well across the board! Then I spent a lot of time refining the OBS, which is very much a give-and-take process requiring another mountain of simulations looking at very specific actions and hands.

While there is a lot of data here, some critics will no doubt say it's not enough. To them I say, feel free to run extra simulations. Or, as Dominator says, "Feel free to go away!" Speed Count is a standard part of all our blackjack training products now, including our own simulator *Blackjack Audit*, so anyone can replicate this data and complete more tests. Over time, I'm sure other simulators will be able to complete these tests too. My goal in this section is provide **average** players with content to help them understand: how much money they will make in different games, the risk, the bankroll requirements, and characteristics of Speed Count.

Details, and Understanding the Tables

Behind every single row or result in the following tables is a simulation run of at least 100 million rounds. We used a $5 unit bet size, 75 percent penetration in all four or more deck games, 67 percent penetration in all double-deck games, and 50 percent penetration in all single-deck games. Generally, we simulated all permutations of: one and six players, DAS/noDAS, S17/H17, 1/2/4/6/8 decks. This makes 2 * 2 * 2 * 5 = 40 different base simulations for every thing we wanted to test. These are reflected in the 40 rows you will tend to see over and over again in these tables. Other minor blackjack rules we assumed are: re-splitting of aces allowed, no hitting split aces (one extra card only), up to two splits (three hands), and dealer peeks for blackjack when dealt 10 up.

Win rate refers to the average number of bet units won per round dealt. To convert this into an hourly win rate, multiply by your unit bet size and expected rounds per hour, historically chosen to be 100.

Avg. bet refers to the average total wagers per round. This is slightly higher than the average bet size per hand, due to splits and doubles. Note that we used a $5 unit bet size for all simulations. Simply multiply accordingly for higher unit bet sizes. It is important to know the difference between unit bet size and average bet size. A $10 player is one whose minimum bet size is $10, not his average bet size.

SD is the standard deviation per round of win/loss, per unit bet. Again, this is slightly different from the standard deviation per betting event or hand, due to splits and doubles. Standard deviation is a reflection of the variability of win or loss, or risk. A higher standard deviation means you will have more fluctuation in your bankroll as you play. We cover bankroll and Risk of Ruin more on page 67.

Exp. is the expectation for this game. Expectation is the average amount of each bet you should expect to win back, over time. Not surprisingly, expectation times the average bet size will be the same as the win rate. When we quote an expectation value from a simulation, it is computed as the sum of all profit or loss divided by the sum of all bets. Some older blackjack books exclude splits and doubles from their expectation values, but we do not.

Conservative Speed Count Performance

plyrs	decks	DAS	H17	win rate	avg. bet	SD	exp.
1	1	noDAS	H17	0.005606	$8.3430	1.90053	0.3360%
1	1	DAS	H17	0.007739	$8.4030	1.92113	0.4605%
1	1	DAS	S17	0.010180	$8.3560	1.90927	0.6091%
1	1	noDAS	S17	0.007995	$8.2900	1.88801	0.4822%
6	1	noDAS	H17	0.004743	$7.5700	1.72530	0.3132%
6	1	DAS	H17	0.006663	$7.6240	1.74352	0.4370%
6	1	DAS	S17	0.009000	$7.6050	1.73806	0.5918%
6	1	noDAS	S17	0.006953	$7.5330	1.71575	0.4615%
1	2	noDAS	H17	0.004720	$11.3370	2.74435	0.2082%
1	2	DAS	H17	0.007856	$11.4270	2.77863	0.3437%
1	2	DAS	S17	0.011103	$11.3090	2.75265	0.4909%
1	2	noDAS	S17	0.008139	$11.2270	2.72023	0.3625%
6	2	noDAS	H17	0.003479	$10.1790	2.50638	0.1709%
6	2	DAS	H17	0.006206	$10.2570	2.53680	0.3025%
6	2	DAS	S17	0.009420	$10.2090	2.52478	0.4614%
6	2	noDAS	S17	0.006701	$10.1360	2.49565	0.3305%
1	4	noDAS	H17	0.001893	$12.0630	3.02535	0.0785%
1	4	DAS	H17	0.005233	$12.1580	3.06474	0.2152%
1	4	DAS	S17	0.008715	$11.9260	3.01191	0.3654%
1	4	noDAS	S17	0.005487	$11.8400	2.97495	0.2317%
6	4	noDAS	H17	0.000772	$10.8450	2.75872	0.0356%
6	4	DAS	H17	0.003635	$10.9110	2.78984	0.1666%
6	4	DAS	S17	0.007267	$10.8260	2.76808	0.3356%
6	4	noDAS	S17	0.004449	$10.7640	2.73825	0.2067%
1	6	noDAS	H17	0.004085	$14.6060	4.30502	0.1398%
1	6	DAS	H17	0.007932	$14.7070	4.35944	0.2697%
1	6	DAS	S17	0.011992	$14.2470	4.24718	0.4209%
1	6	noDAS	S17	0.008253	$14.1580	4.19718	0.2915%
6	6	noDAS	H17	0.000335	$12.6140	3.81872	0.0133%
6	6	DAS	H17	0.004141	$12.6670	3.85703	0.1635%
6	6	DAS	S17	0.007887	$12.4990	3.81072	0.3155%
6	6	noDAS	S17	0.004453	$12.4480	3.77374	0.1789%
1	8	noDAS	H17	0.002451	$15.8170	4.86348	0.0775%
1	8	DAS	H17	0.006842	$15.9150	4.92350	0.2149%
1	8	DAS	S17	0.011572	$15.2810	4.76281	0.3786%
1	8	noDAS	S17	0.007339	$15.1950	4.70755	0.2415%
6	8	noDAS	H17	-0.000252	$13.2350	4.20617	-0.0095%
6	8	DAS	H17	0.003120	$13.2780	4.24529	0.1175%
6	8	DAS	S17	0.007493	$13.0490	4.17924	0.2871%
6	8	noDAS	S17	0.004005	$13.0070	4.14132	0.1539%

To understand how to use these tables, let's look at an example. Suppose you are playing a two deck DAS/S17 blackjack game at a fairly full table, and your minimum bet size is $25. Looking down the table at the 15th row, we see the matching game with six players. Going across, we see that the win rate is 0.009420 bet units per round. Let's suppose that we will play 60 rounds an hour (100 is too high, since there are lot of players at the table). Then our hourly win rate will be: 60 x 0.009420 x $25 = $14.13/hour. Our edge is 0.4614 percent, which tells us, on average, what we can expect to earn off every bet. Earlier in the book we often quoted an hourly win rate for a $10 player of about $7.50 an hour. We can derive that figure from these tables as follows: the win rate for the two-deck game, DAS/H17, heads up play is 0.007856, times 100 hands an hour, time $10 for the bet size, equals $7.86 per hour. For a six deck DAS/S17 game, assuming a full table of six players, we get a win rate from the table of 0.007887, which is an hourly win rate of $7.89 assuming 100 hands per hour for a $10 bettor.

Note that all games have a positive player edge, except for the one absolutely worst game (8 player, noDAS, H17). Excluding single-deck games, I simply move on to the next casino if I can't get DAS and S17, unless there is unusually good penetration or some other advantageous rule (such as surrender). My favorite game, two-deck/DAS/S17/67 percent penetration, delivers an approximately healthy 0.5 percent edge, with the equivalent six-deck game close behind. And this is using the very low bet spread of Speed Count Conservative.

Very Aggressive Speed Count Performance

plyrs	decks	DAS	H17	win rate	avg. bet	SD	exp.
1	1	noDAS	H17	0.024598	$12.4140	3.17941	0.9908%
1	1	DAS	H17	0.027756	$12.4850	3.20652	1.1116%
1	1	DAS	S17	0.031100	$12.3670	3.17071	1.2574%
1	1	noDAS	S17	0.028084	$12.2740	3.14361	1.1441%
6	1	noDAS	H17	0.035334	$12.5480	3.29473	1.3739%
6	1	DAS	H17	0.038344	$12.6000	3.31701	1.4877%
6	1	DAS	S17	0.041232	$12.5490	3.29557	1.6243%
6	1	noDAS	S17	0.038154	$12.4180	3.26171	1.5178%
1	2	noDAS	H17	0.019322	$14.3800	3.72191	0.6718%
1	2	DAS	H17	0.023314	$14.4710	3.75972	0.8056%
1	2	DAS	S17	0.026905	$14.2500	3.70103	0.9440%
1	2	noDAS	S17	0.023101	$14.1680	3.66581	0.8152%
6	2	noDAS	H17	0.022732	$14.1020	3.74732	0.8060%
6	2	DAS	H17	0.026423	$14.1680	3.77937	0.9325%
6	2	DAS	S17	0.030455	$14.0680	3.74746	1.0824%
6	2	noDAS	S17	0.026827	$14.0070	3.71680	0.9576%
1	4	noDAS	H17	0.020224	$20.5060	6.03466	0.4931%
1	4	DAS	H17	0.025895	$20.6240	6.09862	0.6278%
1	4	DAS	S17	0.031175	$20.0090	5.94473	0.7790%
1	4	noDAS	S17	0.025932	$19.9050	5.88520	0.6514%
6	4	noDAS	H17	0.024033	$19.8470	5.99180	0.6054%
6	4	DAS	H17	0.029278	$19.9070	6.04342	0.7354%
6	4	DAS	S17	0.034498	$19.6290	5.96354	0.8788%
6	4	noDAS	S17	0.029679	$19.5760	5.91496	0.7580%
1	6	noDAS	H17	0.019863	$22.2000	7.65193	0.4474%
1	6	DAS	H17	0.025895	$22.3000	7.72957	0.5806%
1	6	DAS	S17	0.031774	$21.3560	7.46807	0.7439%
1	6	noDAS	S17	0.025966	$21.2710	7.39683	0.6104%
6	6	noDAS	H17	0.020576	$20.9820	7.43837	0.4903%
6	6	DAS	H17	0.026020	$21.0010	7.49397	0.6195%
6	6	DAS	S17	0.032010	$20.5880	7.36594	0.7774%
6	6	noDAS	S17	0.026544	$20.5710	7.31279	0.6452%
1	8	noDAS	H17	0.013704	$23.8000	8.15145	0.2879%
1	8	DAS	H17	0.020203	$23.9010	8.23618	0.4226%
1	8	DAS	S17	0.026395	$22.7420	7.92802	0.5803%
1	8	noDAS	S17	0.020102	$22.6550	7.85007	0.4436%
6	8	noDAS	H17	0.015621	$22.1640	7.83288	0.3524%
6	8	DAS	H17	0.021322	$22.1680	7.89139	0.4809%
6	8	DAS	S17	0.027389	$21.6650	7.74281	0.6321%
6	8	noDAS	S17	0.021815	$21.6610	7.68652	0.5036%

The Very Aggressive Speed Count variant improves your earnings substantially by increasing the bets you make when you have a positive edge over the casino. For example, our win rate in the two deck/DAS/S17/1 player game was

0.011103 units with Speed Count Conservative, and is 0.026905 with Very Aggressive. If you are a $10 player, then that's a difference in hourly win rate of $11 for the Speed Count Conservative compared to $26.90 with Speed Count Very Aggressive in this specific game (2.5 times better, assuming 100 rounds per hour).

Of course, this extra performance comes with increased risk and bankroll requirements. We show you bankroll requirements for Speed Count on page 145.

Following the tables in the chapter Betting Your Count, we can see that Speed Count Very Aggressive calls for a bet spread of 1 to 15 units in a two deck game (top bet of three hands of 5 units at a Speed Count of 36). This is definitely very aggressive, and exactly the kind of action that will get the pit bosses scrutinizing your play. All the same, I personally will use an even higher bet spread for very short hit-and-run sessions at casinos with very good double-deck penetration. After an exceptionally big win after multiple high bets, I check my watch and suddenly discover that it's time to catch up with friends… to the cage and homeward bound! Playing advantage blackjack with a 1 percent edge or more is exceptionally fun, but like most high-risk sports, best to fulfill in small bursts. And of course, I always play with a substantial session bankroll at all times. I cringe and caution students when, ripe with the excitement of learning card counting, they declare they're off to beat the casinos with a couple hundred bucks in their pockets. Bad idea.

Aggressive Speed Count Performance

plyrs	decks	DAS	H17	win rate	avg. bet	SD	exp.
1	1	noDAS	H17	0.012403	$9.0560	2.11986	0.6848%
1	1	DAS	H17	0.014753	$9.1170	2.14113	0.8091%
1	1	DAS	S17	0.017232	$9.0590	2.12604	0.9511%
1	1	noDAS	S17	0.014916	$8.9900	2.10332	0.8296%
6	1	noDAS	H17	0.010321	$8.1390	1.92296	0.6340%
6	1	DAS	H17	0.012429	$8.1910	1.94161	0.7586%
6	1	DAS	S17	0.014852	$8.1690	1.93450	0.9091%
6	1	noDAS	S17	0.012664	$8.0910	1.91001	0.7825%
1	2	noDAS	H17	0.011364	$11.9310	2.88853	0.4762%
1	2	DAS	H17	0.014614	$12.0180	2.92254	0.6080%
1	2	DAS	S17	0.017955	$11.8870	2.89176	0.7552%
1	2	noDAS	S17	0.014863	$11.8080	2.85979	0.6294%
6	2	noDAS	H17	0.009394	$10.7410	2.65636	0.4373%
6	2	DAS	H17	0.012368	$10.8160	2.68642	0.5718%
6	2	DAS	S17	0.015685	$10.7620	2.67190	0.7287%
6	2	noDAS	S17	0.012763	$10.6930	2.64324	0.5968%
1	4	noDAS	H17	0.011563	$16.7280	4.59585	0.3456%
1	4	DAS	H17	0.016330	$16.8460	4.65328	0.4847%
1	4	DAS	S17	0.020943	$16.4590	4.56665	0.6362%
1	4	noDAS	S17	0.016397	$16.3540	4.51322	0.5013%
6	4	noDAS	H17	0.009505	$14.7200	4.16927	0.3228%
6	4	DAS	H17	0.013453	$14.7890	4.21323	0.4548%
6	4	DAS	S17	0.018164	$14.6490	4.17752	0.6200%
6	4	noDAS	S17	0.014333	$14.5850	4.13570	0.4914%
1	6	noDAS	H17	0.012387	$17.8210	5.63668	0.3475%
1	6	DAS	H17	0.017102	$17.9280	5.70345	0.4770%
1	6	DAS	S17	0.022002	$17.3000	5.54402	0.6359%
1	6	noDAS	S17	0.017437	$17.2080	5.48317	0.5067%
6	6	noDAS	H17	0.007258	$15.2130	4.98587	0.2385%
6	6	DAS	H17	0.011921	$15.2580	5.03166	0.3906%
6	6	DAS	S17	0.016298	$15.0330	4.96673	0.5421%
6	6	noDAS	S17	0.012252	$14.9900	4.92273	0.4087%
1	8	noDAS	H17	0.007545	$18.6920	5.92329	0.2018%
1	8	DAS	H17	0.012800	$18.8020	5.99636	0.3404%
1	8	DAS	S17	0.018430	$18.0490	5.81062	0.5105%
1	8	noDAS	S17	0.013387	$17.9540	5.74334	0.3728%
6	8	noDAS	H17	0.004892	$15.6940	5.18665	0.1559%
6	8	DAS	H17	0.008833	$15.7380	5.23565	0.2806%
6	8	DAS	S17	0.013982	$15.4660	5.15936	0.4520%
6	8	noDAS	S17	0.009719	$15.4240	5.11201	0.3151%

This strategy is an attempt to sit in between the extremes of Conservative and Very Aggressive Speed Count. But the reality is that all players should experiment with their own variations of Speed Count to find out what method delivers the performance they want, with acceptable bankroll risk, and the least attraction of casino heat. There is no right way to bet or play, as long as you are betting more than your unit bet size above counts of 30, and as little as possible below 31. There is sometimes a lot of discussion about optimal bet spreads, which I still find very strange outside of the ivory towers of blackjack academia. The optimal bet spread is zero below the bet pivot (31 for Speed Count), and the maximum allowed table bet above it! Of course, pragmatics and real bankrolls constrain this approach. While it is true that betting a rational spread of 1/2/4/6/8 will obviously perform better than 1/1/1/8, the reality is that what you bet above the pivot should be what you can afford and what you can get away with in the casino. Applying Kelly Criterion [betting a percentage of your total bankroll based on percentage of edge] for optimal betting (or similar) is nice in principle, but impractical in today's casinos that scrutinize every big bet and unusual play.

The only difference from Speed Count Aggressive and Very Aggressive is the absence of hand spreading. We use the slighter higher bet spread, exit on rotten counts, and insure at high counts. This lowers our risk and bankroll requirement substantially, while still delivering improved win rates. The double-deck/DAS/S17/1 player game we examined earlier has a win rate of 0.017955, which works out to about $18 per hour win rate for the $10 player (Conservative Speed Count yielded $11, while Very Aggressive was $26.90).

As you mix and match to come up with your own Speed Count strategy, just remember to increase your bet above the pivot in some gradual spread, try to not play hands (or just leave the shoe) when the count dives below the starting count, and press those bets when the count sky rockets in the high 30s or 40s. Make sure you play with the right bankroll for your game to maintain no more than five percent risk of ruin, and you're on the way to winning at blackjack.

Bankroll: Conservative Speed Count

plyrs	decks	DAS	H17	LROR	trip: 400	trip: 1200	trip: 4000
1	1	noDAS	H17	$4,826	$363	$618	$1,084
1	1	DAS	H17	$3,572	$364	$614	$1,064
1	1	DAS	S17	$2,682	$358	$597	$1,016
1	1	noDAS	S17	$3,339	$357	$600	$1,037
6	1	noDAS	H17	$4,701	$331	$563	$992
6	1	DAS	H17	$3,417	$331	$559	$971
6	1	DAS	S17	$2,514	$326	$545	$933
6	1	noDAS	S17	$3,171	$325	$548	$948
1	2	noDAS	H17	$11,951	$531	$908	$1,622
1	2	DAS	H17	$7,361	$532	$906	$1,596
1	2	DAS	S17	$5,111	$522	$879	$1,527
1	2	noDAS	S17	$6,809	$519	$885	$1,549
6	2	noDAS	H17	$13,522	$486	$832	$1,492
6	2	DAS	H17	$7,766	$488	$831	$1,472
6	2	DAS	S17	$5,068	$480	$812	$1,411
6	2	noDAS	S17	$6,961	$478	$813	$1,435
1	4	noDAS	H17	$36,202	$590	$1,017	$1,847
1	4	DAS	H17	$13,443	$591	$1,014	$1,812
1	4	DAS	S17	$7,796	$575	$979	$1,721
1	4	noDAS	S17	$12,081	$575	$982	$1,752
6	4	noDAS	H17	$73,793	$541	$933	$1,694
6	4	DAS	H17	$16,037	$541	$928	$1,668
6	4	DAS	S17	$7,897	$530	$903	$1,597
6	4	noDAS	S17	$12,621	$530	$906	$1,621
1	6	noDAS	H17	$33,976	$838	$1,444	$2,605
1	6	DAS	H17	$17,944	$841	$1,442	$2,576
1	6	DAS	S17	$11,265	$814	$1,381	$2,432
1	6	noDAS	S17	$15,986	$808	$1,382	$2,467
6	6	noDAS	H17	$326,394	$747	$1,295	$2,361
6	6	DAS	H17	$26,906	$749	$1,288	$2,326
6	6	DAS	S17	$13,789	$734	$1,253	$2,236
6	6	noDAS	S17	$23,950	$731	$1,257	$2,269
1	8	noDAS	H17	$72,290	$949	$1,642	$2,974
1	8	DAS	H17	$26,535	$953	$1,639	$2,941
1	8	DAS	S17	$14,681	$914	$1,559	$2,760
1	8	noDAS	S17	$22,613	$911	$1,563	$2,794
6	8	noDAS	H17	N/A	N/A	N/A	N/A
6	8	DAS	H17	$43,261	$827	$1,426	$2,577
6	8	DAS	S17	$17,457	$806	$1,381	$2,464
6	8	noDAS	S17	$32,075	$807	$1,386	$2,498

If I could put a flashing light and 'READ ME' alert on these bankroll tables to make sure readers visit them, I would. In all my experience teaching students card counting, the biggest mistake is not playing with enough money. Hopefully you've picked this up in the book by now, and will come to these tables to find out exactly how much money you need to play with to not go broke (or at least, lower this probability). Or better yet, invest in software that includes the bankroll assessment and analysis tools, such as *Blackjack Counter* and *Audit* from our own company.

LROR refers to Lifetime Risk of Ruin, and means the amount of money you should set aside to play for your entire blackjack career, and have no more than 5 percent chance of losing it.

Trip ROR refers to the amount of money you should bring for a single outing or session of blackjack, such as a weekend trip or evening of playing. The required trip bankroll depends on how long you want to play. Presuming 100 hands per hour, the 1200 column above might represent a typical weekend outing of 12 hours or 1200 rounds of play, 400 an average evening session of four hours of play, and 4000 a week of playing.

The previous tables assume the same game characteristics we've outlined before. Also, they are computing the 5 percent Risk of Ruin bankroll values (the bankroll required to have at most 5 percent chance of losing that money playing). More importantly, note that the dollar amounts above assume a $5 unit bet size. So let's say your unit bet size (minimum bet size) is $25, and you're playing that sweet double-deck/DAS/S17/1 player game. Looking at the 11th row, we can see that the 'one night' 500 round trip ROR is $522 for a $5 bettor. Hence, for a $25 bettor we should not go play that night with less than 5 x $522 = approximately $2500 session bankroll to minimize the risk of going broke (he will have only a 5 percent chance of walking out broke as a $25 player). Want to last over the long haul as a for-profit player... better stash away $5000 x 5 = $25,000 in a 401-G right from the start. Only by doing so will you be able to manage the inevitable swings and occasional losing streaks that are bound to happen. These are sobering bankroll amounts for most new card counters.

Bankroll: Very Aggressive Speed Count

plyrs	decks	DAS	H17	LROR	trip: 400	trip: 1200	trip: 4000
1	1	noDAS	H17	$3,078	$583	$959	$1,575
1	1	DAS	H17	$2,774	$583	$954	$1,550
1	1	DAS	S17	$2,421	$570	$927	$1,476
1	1	noDAS	S17	$2,635	$569	$932	$1,503
6	1	noDAS	H17	$2,358	$590	$949	$1,502
6	1	DAS	H17	$2,198	$588	$945	$1,477
6	1	DAS	S17	$1,995	$579	$920	$1,411
6	1	noDAS	S17	$2,114	$578	$925	$1,437
1	2	noDAS	H17	$5,369	$698	$1,170	$1,993
1	2	DAS	H17	$4,541	$699	$1,162	$1,951
1	2	DAS	S17	$3,813	$682	$1,125	$1,862
1	2	noDAS	S17	$4,357	$681	$1,132	$1,898
6	2	noDAS	H17	$4,627	$696	$1,161	$1,952
6	2	DAS	H17	$4,049	$696	$1,155	$1,914
6	2	DAS	S17	$3,454	$685	$1,123	$1,835
6	2	noDAS	S17	$3,857	$686	$1,130	$1,876
1	4	noDAS	H17	$13,486	$1,149	$1,949	$3,411
1	4	DAS	H17	$10,757	$1,151	$1,944	$3,362
1	4	DAS	S17	$8,490	$1,111	$1,866	$3,184
1	4	noDAS	S17	$10,003	$1,109	$1,866	$3,224
6	4	noDAS	H17	$11,188	$1,137	$1,912	$3,322
6	4	DAS	H17	$9,343	$1,136	$1,907	$3,266
6	4	DAS	S17	$7,721	$1,112	$1,855	$3,137
6	4	noDAS	S17	$8,829	$1,112	$1,863	$3,190
1	6	noDAS	H17	$22,077	$1,466	$2,501	$4,420
1	6	DAS	H17	$17,280	$1,473	$2,498	$4,371
1	6	DAS	S17	$13,146	$1,412	$2,375	$4,108
1	6	noDAS	S17	$15,781	$1,406	$2,381	$4,161
6	6	noDAS	H17	$20,139	$1,426	$2,419	$4,268
6	6	DAS	H17	$16,165	$1,425	$2,415	$4,215
6	6	DAS	S17	$12,695	$1,389	$2,343	$4,042
6	6	noDAS	S17	$15,088	$1,389	$2,350	$4,096
1	8	noDAS	H17	$36,313	$1,578	$2,695	$4,823
1	8	DAS	H17	$25,147	$1,584	$2,695	$4,764
1	8	DAS	S17	$17,834	$1,507	$2,560	$4,476
1	8	noDAS	S17	$22,959	$1,502	$2,567	$4,529
6	8	noDAS	H17	$29,416	$1,508	$2,586	$4,596
6	8	DAS	H17	$21,874	$1,512	$2,574	$4,529
6	8	DAS	S17	$16,393	$1,473	$2,498	$4,355
6	8	noDAS	S17	$20,283	$1,471	$2,496	$4,398

The Very Aggressive Speed Count bankroll tables are well worth examining in detail. Not surprisingly, you will find that you need a lot more money to play aggressively.

But let's take a closer look at the Lifetime Risk of Ruin for our favorite double-deck/DAS/S17 one player game (row 11). In the table on page 142 we saw that $522 was required for a typical evening playing session at $5 dollar tables. Referring to the previous tables, we see that the equivalent bankroll for Speed Count Very Aggressive is $682, which is substantially higher as expected. But the 5 percent lifetime risk of ruin bankroll is $3,813, which is substantially lower than the equivalent $5,111 bankroll for Speed Count Conservative! How can that be?

Risk of ruin is a complex mathematical property, which depends on much more than just the standard deviation (or variance). It also factors in your win rate. So while Speed Count Very Aggressive clearly has a higher variance due to the increased bets, it also produces better earnings. In the long run (lifetime risk of ruin), the improved performance pays off and actually **lowers** our risk, while making us more money, clearly the best of both worlds, as long as we bring enough money to the tables every time we play, and the casino doesn't give us the boot for our aggressive playing style.

We're not including bankroll tables for Speed Count Aggressive (our 'middle of the road' strategy), since we've already noted that it's a matter of personal taste and comfort to tune Speed Count the way you like it. If you want to find out the right bankroll or risk for your own favorite game and parameters, I strongly advise you to invest in some simulation and analysis blackjack software that includes ROR tools (**www.HandheldBlackjack.com**).

During the course of developing Speed Count, I generated a ton of additional simulation data that is not provided in this book. But hopefully you get the point, namely, that Speed Count is not only easy to learn and use, it has the power to give you the edge over the casino when you play blackjack. Now that's exciting!

- Appendix III -
How to Play Blackjack

Objective of the Game

The objective of blackjack is to beat the dealer's hand by either, 1) having your hand total higher than the dealer's hand or, 2) by not going over 21 when the dealer does (exceeding a total of 21 is known as "busting").

Card Values

All cards count their face value in blackjack. Picture cards count as 10 and the ace can count as either a 1 or 11. Card suits have no meaning in blackjack. The total of any hand is the sum of the card values in the hand. A hand containing a 4-5-8 totals 17. Another containing a queen-5 totals 15. It is always assumed that the ace counts as 11 unless your hand exceeds 21 in which case the ace reverts to a value of 1.

Soft Hands and Hard Hands

Any hand which contain an ace that counts as 11 is known as a soft hand (i.e., ace-7 is a soft 18 hand and ace-3-3 is soft 17). A hard hand is any hand that either does *not* contain an ace, or if it does, it counts as 1 (i.e., 10-8 and 5-ace-10-2 are hard 18 hands). Soft hands are played differently than hard hands.

Number of Players

Blackjack tables can accommodate from one up to six or seven players. All players are competing against the casino dealer's hand and not against each other's hands. The cards are always dealt by the casino dealer.

Playing With Chips

Casinos prefer that players bet with casino chips (also known as cheques) rather than with cash (in some gaming jurisdictions it's forbidden to bet with cash). To convert your cash to casino chips wait until the dealer completes the hand in progress and then place your cash on the layout above your betting spot (otherwise the cash could be mistaken for a bet on the next hand). The dealer will exchange your cash for an equivalent amount of casino chips, which you can place in front of you. (Note that some casinos don't allow players to enter mid-game. If this is the case, wait till the dealer finishes the shoe and begins to reshuffle before you place your cash on the table for chips).

Marker Play

Instead of bringing cash to the table to play, you can take a marker. This is an IUO that you sign to receive casino chips. In order to take a marker, you must have filled out a credit application beforehand with the casino and be approved. Contact the casino's marketing department for details on completing a credit application (or visit the casino's web site for details).

Betting Limits

Before you sit down at a blackjack table, make sure you know what the table betting limits are. There is usually a small display on the table (on the dealer's right side) that will tell you the table minimum and maximum betting limits. A table that has a $10 minimum betting requirement means that you must wager at least $10 (or more) on each hand. If a table has a $1,000 table maximum betting limit this means you are not allowed to make your initial wager more than $1,000. You are permitted in most casinos to wager more than one spot but the casinos usually require you to bet twice the table minimum on both hands.

Number of Decks

Generally from one to eight-decks are used to play blackjack. Single-deck games are dealt by hand. Double-deck games are usually dealt by hand but some casinos use a device known as a card shoe to hold the undealt cards and the dealer will deal the cards from this shoe. A shoe is also used in 4, 6 and 8 deck games.

The Deal

Prior to the deal of the cards, all players must make a bet by placing chips in their respective betting spots. Every player and the dealer will receive two cards. One of the dealer's cards (known as the dealer's upcard or face card) is dealt up so that players can see its value. The other dealer's card (known as the dealer's downcard or hole card) is unseen. The two player cards can be dealt either face up, face down, or sometimes one up and one down. In general when games are dealt from dealing shoes (normally containing four, six or eight-decks of cards) the player's cards are dealt face up. In this case you should not handle the cards. In games in which the dealer deals from the hand by pitching the cards to the players (single or double-deck games) the player cards are usually dealt both face down. When the cards are dealt face up, it is permissible for the player to handle the cards (with *one hand* only and the cards must always be above the table).

Blackjacks

When a player is dealt an ace and a 10-valued card as his first two cards, it is called a "blackjack" or "natural" and generally is paid one and one-half times the original bet (i.e., a 3 to 2 payoff). Some casinos pay 6 to 5 on player blackjacks which gives the casino a higher edge over players.

Push

When your hand totals the same as the dealer this is known as a push or tie and you get to retain the bet (i.e., you don't lose your bet on tied hands).

Player's Action

If the dealer doesn't have a blackjack, players have to make a decision on how they want to play their hand. Player's options include the following:

Hit

This means you want the dealer to give you another card to your hand. You must use a hand signal to signify to the dealer that you want another card. In face up games, if you want a hit, make a beckoning motion with your finger, or tap the table behind your cards with your finger. In face down games, scratch the edges of the cards in your hand lightly on the felt.

Stand

This means you are satisfied with the total of the hand and want to stand with the cards you have. In face up games, indicate that you want to stand by waving your hand over the cards. In face down games, tuck your cards under the chips that you wagered in your betting spot.

Doubling Down

This playing option allows you to double your bet in return for receiving one and only one draw card. You can only double down after you receive your first two cards and before drawing another card. To signal the dealer that you want to double down just place your chip next to the original chip bet on the hand. In face down games you must also toss your cards face up in front of you on the layout and then make the secondary double down bet as above. Most casinos allow players to double for less which means you can wager less than the original bet when you make the secondary double down bet. In a face up game, the draw card on a double down is usually placed perpendicular to the initial two cards. In a face down game, the dealer will usually place the draw card face down in front of you (however in some casinos it is dealt face up).

Pair Splitting

If you have two like cards (e.g., a pair of 6's or aces), you could exercise the option to split. When you split you must make another bet equal to your original bet (just place your chip next to the original chip bet on the hand). By pair splitting you play each card as a separate hand and you can draw as many cards as you like to each hand (except split aces-most casinos will only allow one draw card to each ace). For example, if you were dealt a pair of 8's (16) and split, you would have two separate hands containing an 8. You would be required to play out one of the split hands first before taking any action on the other hand. In face up games you indicate that you want to split by placing another chip next to the original chip. For face down games toss your cards on the table and then make the secondary wager. Most casinos will allow players to split all 10 value cards such as a jack-ten or queen-king (although this is not a recommended playing strategy). Also most casinos will allow a player to resplit up to a total of 3 or 4 hands (e.g., if you are dealt a pair of 8's, split and you draw another 8 to one hand you can resplit again). Most casinos also allow players to double down after pair splitting (this is a player favorable rule). Keep in mind that if you split aces and receive a ten to an ace you have a 21 and not a blackjack.

Surrender

Some but not all casinos allow this option. Surrender allows a player to forfeit their initial hand with an automatic loss of half the original bet. Players can surrender their initial two card hand only after the dealer has checked his cards for a blackjack. Once a player draws a third card the surrender option is no longer available. If the dealer has a blackjack hand, then surrender is not available. When a player surrenders (to do so tell the dealer "surrender") the dealer will remove the player's card from the table and place one half of the players bet in the chip rack. The player is no longer involved in that round. In some casinos a hand signal must be given for surrender, which is to use your finger and draw an imaginary line from left to right across the felt layout.

Insurance

When the dealer's upcard is an ace, the dealer will ask players if they want to make the insurance wager. Insurance is a side bet in which players are betting that the dealer's hole card will be a ten-value card. Players can make an insurance bet equal to one half of the initial bet made on the hand. To make the insurance bet you simply place your chips on the insurance line, which is located right above the player betting spot. You win your insurance bet if the dealer has a ten-value card in the hole. A winning insurance bet pays off at 2 to 1 odds.

Even Money

When the player has a blackjack hand and the dealer has an ace showing the dealer will ask the player if he wants "even money." Even money means the dealer will automatically give you a 1 to 1 (or even money) payoff on your bet before he checks his hole card for a potential blackjack. Taking even money yields the same result as making an insurance bet on your blackjack hand.

Busting

If a player's hand exceeds a total of 21, he automatically busts and loses the hand. When a player busts, his cards and his bet are immediately collected by the dealer. This is how the casino has the mathematical edge over players. If a player busts he loses even if the dealer subsequently busts in the same round.

Dealer's Play

Unlike players, the dealer in blackjack has no playing option. Casino rules specify that a dealer must draw when the dealer's hand totals less than 17 and stand when the total is 17 to 21. In some casinos, dealers must stand on soft 17 and in others they must hit (it's better for the player if the rules specify the dealer must *stand* on soft 17).

Shuffle Machines

Most casinos use automatic shufflers to shuffle the cards in multiple deck games. Usually the dealer will use say six decks of cards while a different set of six-decks of cards is being shuffled offline by an automatic shuffling device. When the cut card appears, the dealer will complete that round and then switch the two sets of cards (i.e., the off line shuffled decks of cards are put into play while the just used set of cards are placed in the automatic shuffler to be shuffled). Automatic shufflers eliminate the downtime that occurs when the dealer manually shuffles the cards. Another type of automatic shuffler is known as a continuous shuffling machine (CSM). With this device the discards from one round are placed back into the shuffler to be mixed with the undealt decks of cards. With a CSM, there is never a pause in action and more hands are dealt per hour than with an automatic shuffler.

– Appendix IV –
Golden Touch Blackjack Course

You have now read the book with the easiest advantage-play blackjack method ever developed. Most blackjack players assume that they will now stay at home and practice until they are good enough to go into the casinos and beat the game of blackjack. Sadly most of these players are wrong. While practicing at home is a praiseworthy desire, many players just don't have the time to put in such intense practice or they lack the discipline to stick to a strong training regimen.

For those of you who want to learn Speed Count and the Optimum Basic Strategy in just two days from veteran pros Frank Scoblete and Henry Tamburin, you should take the Golden Touch Blackjack class. In our class we teach you in a simulated casino environment with intense hands-on instruction, how to master Speed Count and the Optimum Basic Strategy so that you can feel 100 percent confident in its use in the casino environment.

Why not learn directly from the professionals who created Speed Count and have used it in the casinos with wonderful success?

Give yourself two days to really get good so that every time you step into the casino you'll know that you have them where they wish they had you. How many players can say that?

The Golden Touch Blackjack hands-on course is for you if:

- You desire to learn the technique in two days of intense training under the supervision of real blackjack professionals.

- You are a casino player who would like to learn the game of blackjack and learn a technique that will give you the edge in just two days of practice.

- You are a blackjack player who has tried and failed to master traditional card counting but still want to play with a good edge.

- You are a blackjack player who finds counting cards to be laborious and exhausting but you are looking for an easier way to get the edge.

- You are a traditional basic strategy player who desires to become an advantage player, without spending countless days, months and years devoted to the learning process.

- You are a player who is looking for an easier system where the trap of counting errors doesn't erase your earnings potential.

- You are an advantage video poker or craps player (a controlled shooter) looking to add another advantage game to your arsenal.

Casino gambling is fun but if you believe that winning is the most fun, then our GTB class is for you. Get the winner's edge in just two days. Sign up for the Golden Touch Blackjack class today!

Visit our web site at:

www.goldentouchblackjack.com
Or, call now: 1-800-944-0406

New! One day Speed Count course

In our traditional two day course, we teach you not only everything about Speed Count, but go into much more depth into practical and important generic blackjack areas such as camouflage, bankroll management, leveraging comps, and much more.

But if you want to save time, **and money**, consider our 1 day shortened Speed Count courses. You get the same intense hands-on training in our simulated casino environment where you play real blackjack under the tutelage of our pro instructions, in a condensed 1 day format.

Visit our web site at:

www.GoldentouchBlackjack.com
Or, call now: 1-800-944-0406

Here is a sampling of feedback from students that attended our Golden Touch Blackjack course (for more visit **www.goldentouchblackjack.com**):

- "This course was even better than I expected."

- "A first rate professionally created and presented course which was comprehensive, well organized, and very enjoyable. Congratulations to everyone involved in discovering SC and teaching it to players."

- "Excellent course, well instructed, with lots of information and ideas."

- "The course should definitely pay for itself by applying the methods. Thank you!"

- "Excellent course. Content is unique and instructors interested in teaching concepts to students from the beginner to the most experienced."

- "The relaxed course atmosphere and the knowledge of the instructors were awesome!"

- "The instructors were excellent and well versed in all the topics discussed in the course. They were also very helpful and patient with students who had a very limited knowledge of blackjack."

- Appendix V -
Golden Touch Blackjack DVD

Don't Have Time for a Class?
Get Our Golden Touch Blackjack DVD!

Not everyone can take the time out of his or her busy schedules to take one of our outstanding hands-on classes. The next best thing is to get our DVD with Dr. Henry Tamburin, Dominator and Frank Scoblete showing you step-by-step how to get the edge at blackjack. This DVD was shot during an actual class and is a truly valuable learning tool for players who want to beat the casinos at their own games.

To get more information, visit our web site at:

www.GoldentouchBlackjack.com
Or, call now: 1-800-944-0406

- Appendix VI -
Optimum Basic Strategy Cards

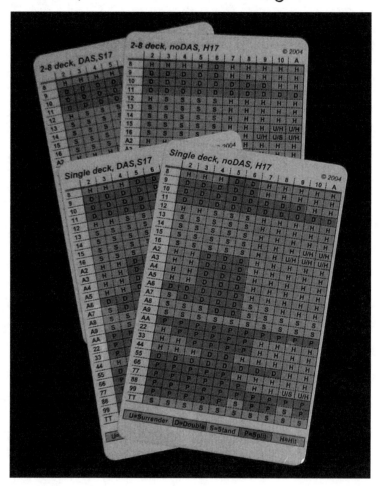

Let them think you are less than what you are! Increase your edge; decrease casino suspicions.

You don't have to memorize the new Optimum Basic Strategy because you can bring the cards to the table with you. There are eight optimum strategies on the four cards, each card designed to increase your edge while using Speed Count in games with various rules.

The cards are the size of a credit card, laminated and in color. They are easy to use.

Remember the OBS cards do several things for you:

1. They make you play 100 percent correctly in all games.
2. They increase your edge over the house while using Speed Count.
3. They make you appear to be less than a basic strategy player.
4. They give you excellent camouflage in the casinos.

One set of four cards (eight strategies) is just $15. If you wish to buy two sets, it is just $25.

To purchase, visit our web site at:
www.GoldenTouchBlackjack.com

Or, call: 1-888-353-3234

Nothing Beats Hands-On Instruction!

Join the Craps Revolution!

Frank Scoblete's

Golden Touch Crap$

<u>Dice Control Seminars!</u>

Are you a winner in business, in your chosen career or profession but a long-term loser at craps? If your answer is yes, it doesn't have to be, because craps can be beaten! It isn't easy and not everyone can do it, but then again, not everyone can be successful in business and life. **If you are interested in beating the game of craps, read on.**

There is only one way to beat craps in the long run and that is to *control the dice* when you shoot so that you *reduce* the appearance of certain numbers and *increase* the appearance of other numbers – thus offsetting the house edge and giving the edge to you, the *skilled* player. Frank Scoblete, gambling's #1 best-selling author, calls such skilled dice-controllers "golden shooters," and they are. Why? Because they have the **Golden Touch!**

Dice control is a **physical skill** that can be learned by disciplined players who are willing to practice and perfect the techniques we teach them in our exclusive **Golden Touch Craps** dice-control seminars. Our teachers are the greatest dice-control specialists in the world, many with books and major publications to their credit, *all with years of winning casino experience behind them!* That's why prominent sports figures, enlightened professionals, and successful businessmen and women take the **Golden Touch** dice-control seminars because **you get what you pay for** with **Golden Touch**:

➢ Intense two-day seminars that cover the **physical elements** of controlled shooting: stance and scanning, set, angle, grab, grip, delivery, spin control, and bounce control!

➢ **Hands-on** small-group workshops **with skilled coaches** who show you how it's done and work side-by-side and step-by-step with you to master these physical elements before moving on!

➢ Strong tutoring in maintaining **mental discipline, focus, centering** and **stamina** for making *your* golden touch last at the table no matter what the distractions!

➢ Betting strategies based on applying **sound mathematical principles**, rather than superstitions, so that your golden touch is not tarnished by poor gambling practices!

➢ How to **maintain your edge while random rollers shoot** based on recent breakthrough, mathematical research!

➢ How to **win the game within the game** of casino craps!

➢ How to assess your edge and **optimize your betting strategies** to exploit it!

As shown on the Travel Channel, A&E, and the History Channel, Golden Touch Dice Control is the most powerful advantage-play method ever developed for the game of craps. Join Frank Scoblete, Dominator, and the Golden Touch Craps dice control crew and learn what the casinos don't want you to know – how to beat them.

Seminars forming now!

**Call us TOLL FREE at 1-866-SET-DICE
or 1-800-944-0406**

Or, visit our web site:

www.goldentouchcraps.com

Golden Touch Craps' Private Web Site

Join **The Golden Touch Craps Club™** and enjoy these Members-Only Features:

Over 5,000 paid members! This is an active board with multiple posts in the following areas:

- ✓ Craps
- ✓ Get-Togethers
- ✓ Casino News
- ✓ Other Games
- ✓ The Good, the Bad and the Mediocre (Casino Reviews)
- ✓ Books
- ✓ Movies
- ✓ Television
- ✓ The World We Live In
- ✓ Coffee Chat Lounge
- ✓ Humor
- ✓ Golden Touch Craps Wisdom
- ✓ Special Announcements
- ✓ Exclusive discounts
- ✓ Articles

Exclusive posts by Golden Touch Dice Control Instructors: Frank Scoblete, Dominator, Howard "Rock 'n Roller," Billy "the Kid," Jerry "Stickman," Bill Burton, Street Dog, Mr. Finesse, Doc Holliday, Daryl "No Field Five," Tenor, Satch, Arman "Pit Boss," Don "Wordslayer," Jake "from Pitt," Fred "Chip," Nick "Lefty" T, and Charlie "Ten-Pin"

Monthly or Discounted 13-Month Memberships

Web site: www.GoldenTouchCraps.com
Or call: 1-866-SET-DICE

The Golden Touch Craps Club™ is an exclusive site. You must supply your name, address, phone, and an active e-mail address. Once you have paid, you will receive a preliminary user name and password. You can change these once you enter the site.

- Appendix VIII -
Blackjack Insider Newsletter

The *Blackjack Insider Newsletter* contains a wealth of information for blackjack players who want to take their game to the next level. Regular features include reports on current playing conditions in different cities, playing strategy articles, tournament playing advice, detailed trip reports from pros, book reviews, tips from industry insiders, a schedule of blackjack tournaments, tips on playing Texas Hold'em, and discounts and promotions on books and software. Well known blackjack and gaming experts contribute to the newsletter including Frank Scoblete, Kenneth Smith, Eliot Jacobson, Kevin Blackwood, Barfarkel, Dan Pronovost, LV Tournament Pro, Bill Burton, Fred Renzey, and others. The newsletter is edited by Henry Tamburin and distributed electronically by e-mail each month to subscribers. You can also view past issues online.

www.bjinsider.com

FREE 3-MONTH MEMBERSHIP

To receive a FREE unlimited 3-month membership visit:

http://www.bjinsider.com/freebji

You membership will entitle you to three monthly issues of the newsletter in which you will be able to read all the articles and reports including those for members-only, plus you will have access to over 200 past articles/reports in the BJI Newsletter archives.

- Appendix IX -
Blackjack Glossary

Here are some blackjack terms that are used in this book.

ace: An ace can count as either 1 or 11. It is always assumed that an ace in your hand counts as 11 unless your hand exceeds 21, in which case the ace reverts to a value of 1.

action: The total amount of money that a player wagers over a period of time.

advantage player: A player who has the mathematical advantage over the casino (for example by card counting).

anchor player: The player seated in third base and the last to act before the dealer acts on his hand.

automatic shuffler machine: A machine used to pre-shuffle a separate shoe of cards, so that it is ready to be used after the current shoe is exhausted.

average bet: The average total amount of player's wagers per round.

back counting: Playing technique in which a player stands behind a table and counts the cards as a spectator with the intent of entering the game once the count becomes player favorable.

backed off: When a casino supervisor, while you are playing blackjack, asks you to stop playing. Generally when you are backed off you are not read the trespass act or barred.

bankroll: The money you bring and use to gamble.

barring: When a casino supervisor tells you that you are permanently prohibited from playing blackjack in the casino.

basic strategy: The mathematically optimum way to play your hand based solely on the player's first two cards and the dealer's upcard. Good basic strategy minimizes the casino's edge over the player.

bet sizing: Scaling the size of your bet in relation to your mathematical advantage over the casino.

bet spread: The range between a player's minimum and maximum bets.

betting spot: Also called the betting circle or square, it's the designated area on the layout in front of a player where the player places his bet.

bet unit: Refers to the amount of your unit bet size. Most blackjack math is done in bet units, to generalize the results for all players (multiply by your unit bet size).

blackjack: When the player's initial two cards consists of an ace and a ten value card. Also called a '21'.

blackjack counter: A player who monitors the dealt cards in some fashion that indicates who has an advantage (the casino or player), and by how much. Counters can use one of many different count systems, which all come down to measuring the disproportionate distribution of remaining cards. Depending on the count and the advantage it indicates, the player will bet more or less money.

blacks: Black colored casino chips worth $100 in denomination.

black chip player: A player who wagers $100 or more per hand.

burn card: After the dealer shuffles the cards and they are cut, it's the top card removed from play.

bust: When a player's hand totals more than 21.

buy-in: The exchange of player's cash for casino chips.

camouflage: Techniques to disguise the fact you are card counting.

card counter: A player who keeps track of specific cards as they played for the purpose of knowing when the odds shift in his favor.

casino hold: For table games, the hold is a percentage of all the player's buy-in that is won by the casino.

comp: A free product or service that the casino extends to their loyal players.

continuous shuffling machine (CSM): A shuffling machine that randomly mixes the discards from each round with the undealt cards. Card counting does not work against a CSM.

count: The value of the Speed Count. Also used to refer to the value of the counting metric with any count system.

cut card: A colored plastic card inserted by the player into the shuffled decks of cards to determine where the dealer will cut the decks. When the cut card appears during a round, the round is completed and then the decks are shuffled.

cutoff: The unplayed cards remaining in the shoe after the cut card appears.

DAS: Double after pair splitting. noDAS means that doubling after splitting is not allowed. DAS in an advantageous rule for the player.

discards: The cards that are removed from a round of play and placed in the discard tray.

discard tray: A clear plastic device that holds the dealt cards during play.

double down: After a player receives his initial two cards, he has the option to make one secondary bet up to the amount of the initial bet and receive exactly one extra dealt card.

early surrender: A player is allowed to surrender their hand *before* the dealer checks for a blackjack (see *Surrender*).

edge: Generally refers to the mathematical advantage as a percentage the casino has over the player or vice versa. The edge is the average amount of each and every bet you make that you should expect to win or lose in the long run.

emotional bankroll: An amount of bankroll that allows a player to take naturally occurring and expected losses in stride.

even money: When the player has a blackjack hand and the dealer has an ace showing, the player has the option to take an even money payoff before the dealer checks his hole card for a blackjack. Taking even money is the same as insuring the hand.

exit strategy: Leaving a blackjack table or not playing rounds when the count is very poor indicating a high house edge.

401-G: A money market account with funds set aside only for gambling.

face down game: The player's initial two cards are dealt face down and the player must handle the cards themselves.

face up game: The player's initial two cards are dealt face up and the player is not permitted to handle or touch the cards.

first base: The player's seat located on the far right of the blackjack table that is dealt first (dealer's left side).

floorman: Casino executive located in the pit and responsible for supervising a group of casino games.

greens: Chips in a casino valued at $25 (typically green).

h17: Dealer must hit soft 17. S17 is a favorable and preferable rule for the player.

hard hand: A hard hand is any hand that either does *not* contain an ace, or if it does, it must count as 1.

heads up: Playing alone with the dealer.

heat: When casino executives scrutinize a player very carefully while he plays.

histogram: A chart using consecutive bars to represent a series of values across a category.

hit: When a player requests another card (or by the rules, a dealer must draw another card).

hole card: The dealer's card that is dealt face down. Also known as the down card.

host: A casino employee that caters to casino players who wager a fair amount in the casino.

insurance: Insurance is a side bet in which players are betting that the dealer's hole card will be a ten-value card. Players can make an insurance bet up to one half of the initial bet made on the hand. You win your insurance bet if the dealer has a ten-value card in the hole. A winning insurance bet pays off at 2 to 1 odds.

ISC: Initial Speed Count or the value of the Speed Count at the start of a new shoe.

lifetime risk of ruin (LROR): The amount of money a player should set aside to play for their entire blackjack career with no more than some fixed chance of losing it (typically chosen to be 5 percent).

marker: A promissory note that can be drawn against your bank account.

mid-shoe entry: A big question is what happens if you place a bet on the felt in the middle of a shoe? Some casinos will not allow you to make a bet if you have not been betting since the start of the shoe. This restriction is designed to hamper card counters from only betting when the count is favorable.

natural: Another name for a blackjack hand. Also called a "21."

nickels: $5 denomination chips.

optimum basic strategy (OBS): A hand playing strategy that is used by a player who uses Speed Count.

pair split: See splitting.

peek: When the dealer is dealt an ace or ten upcard and manually checks the hole card to determine if he has a blackjack. Insurance is offered prior to the peek if the up card is an ace. If the hand is a blackjack, the dealer flips the hand and the round is done.

penetration: The percentage of cards that are dealt before the shuffle.

pivot point: The value of the Speed Count where the player's expectation turns from negative to positive.

pitch: A method used by the dealer to deal the cards to players usually in single and double-deck games.

play variation: A deviation from the basic playing strategy used by advanced card counters based upon the count.

pit: The area in the middle of a grouping of blackjack tables. Casino supervisors who monitor the games are located in the pit.

pit boss: Casino executive responsible for table games.

ploppy: Slang term for an unskilled blackjack player.

progressive betting systems: A method used by players to vary the size of their bets based upon the win/loss result of the previous hand. A betting system, without using card counting, is a good way to lose money (betting systems alone cannot help you win).

push: When a player's hand totals the same as the dealer's hand (also known as a tie).

quarter chips: $25 denomination chips.

quarter player: A player who wagers a minimum of $25 on each hand.

rating: Method used by the pit to keep track of the amount of money wagered by a player for the purpose of establishing a comp value.

reds: Chips in a casino valued at $5 (typically red).

resplits: Allowing a player to resplit a pair, usually limited to 3 or 4 hands.

rule of six: In single-deck games, the number of rounds dealt before the shuffle equals 6 minus the number of players.

risk of ruin: The percentage chance of a player losing his bankroll.

s17: Dealer must stand on all 17's (including soft 17). This rule is advantageous for the player.

session bankroll: Amount of bankroll required for a single sitting of play at a casino game.

shoe: Device used to hold the undealt cards, usually when 4 or more decks of cards are used.

soft hand: A hand containing an ace counted as 11.

speed count: A novel card counting method that tracks the ratio of 2-6's played per hand.

splitting: A player choice available only when your first two cards are a pair, or two ten-valued cards. A new card is dealt to each original card creating a new hand, and the player adds a new bet for the second hand. Each hand is now played separately (including more splits). Dissimilar face cards and tens may be split as well, although it is not generally to the player's advantage and rarely done.

stand: The player's decision not to receive any more cards (or the dealer requirement that he not draw any more cards).

standard deviation: A reflection of the variability of win or loss, or risk. A higher standard deviation means you will have more fluctuation in your bankroll as you play.

stiff: A hard hand that totals 12 through 16.

surrender: A playing option whereby a player can forfeit half of his bet, and the right to complete his hand. You can only surrender after you receive your initial two cards and after the dealer checks if he has a blackjack (also known as *late surrender*).

third base: The playing seat located to the far left of the blackjack table, dealt last before the dealer (to the right of the dealer).

trip bankroll: An amount of bankroll required for a trip (consisting of more than one playing session).

trip risk of ruin (trip ROR): The amount of money a player should bring for a single trip or session of blackjack, such as a weekend trip or evening of playing, to maintain less than a fixed chance risk of losing it (usually 5 percent).

toke: Another term for a dealer tip.

total bankroll: The money a player uses for their entire lifetime of playing blackjack.

unit bet size: The dollar value of your minimum bet.

upcard: The dealer's card (of the two initial cards) that is dealt face up for the players to see.

variability: The ups and downs of your bankroll over time.

win rate: The average number of bet units won per round dealt. To convert this into an hourly win rate, multiply by your unit bet size and expected rounds per hour, generally 100.

- Appendix X -
Index Entries